TEACHING, LEARNING AND COMMUNICATION

NEW PATTERNS OF LEARNING SERIES
EDITED BY P.J. HILLS
UNIVERSITY OF CAMBRIDGE

Teaching, Learning and Communication

P.J. HILLS

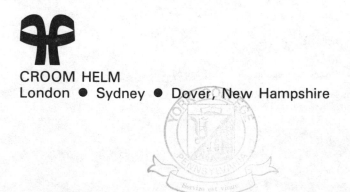

CROOM HELM
London ● Sydney ● Dover, New Hampshire

© 1986 P.J. Hills
Croom Helm Ltd, Provident House, Burrell Row,
Beckenham, Kent BR3 1AT
Croom Helm Australia Pty Ltd, Suite 4, 6th Floor,
64–76 Kippax Street, Surry Hills, NSW 2010 Australia

British Library Cataloguing in Publication Data

Hills, P.J.
  Teaching, learning and communication. — (New
  patterns of learning series)
  1. Communication in education 2. Teaching
  I. Title II. Series
  371.1'022   LB1027
  ISBN 0-7099-4707-0

Croom Helm, 51 Washington Street, Dover, New Hampshire 03820 USA

Library of Congress Cataloging-in-Publication Data applied for.

Filmset by Mayhew Typesetting, Bristol, England

Printed and bound in Great Britain by
Biddles Ltd, Guildford and King's Lynn

CONTENTS

THE PURPOSE OF THIS SERIES

There are now some eighteen books in this series, ranging over many areas of current thinking in education. A list of these will be found at the beginning of this book. These books are of interest to educators, trainers and administrators responsible for the implementation of educational policies in higher, further and continuing education. Each book contains extensive references to key works to enable the reader to pursue selected areas in more depth should he or she wish.

The original version of this book *Teaching and Learning as a Communication Process* (Croom Helm, 1979) was published shortly before the series began. I am pleased therefore to place this version in this successful and expanding series, providing as it does a perspective on the communication process between teacher and student.

P.J. Hills
Cambridge

INTRODUCTION

This book is a revised and expanded version of the text of *Teaching and Learning as a Communication Process*, originally published by Croom Helm in 1979. In the intervening years much has happened both in education and in the world at large.

The increasing pressures for change in the curriculum at all levels of education, developments in micro-computers, computer data bases and in telecommunications generally, coupled with the present state of the economy, are compelling us to take a much more concerned look at the processes underlying teaching and learning. This book, and its two companion volumes *Educating for a Computer Age* and *Educational Futures* (both to be published later this year by Croom Helm), examines these pressures and changes to see how they affect present educational communication processes, and discusses their likely effects in the future.

Although *Teaching, Learning and Communication* concentrates as before on the communication process between teacher and learner, in this version there is more emphasis on the teacher as manager of the learning process and the student as both receiver and communicator. The original version has been found very useful in staff development courses at all levels and as a reference text for those concerned in work with students on communication skills. As a further aid in these areas a comprehensive bibliography on communication skills of speaking, writing, and interactive group processes, has been included, together with sections on teacher and student processes. It is intended that this version will be of use to all those engaged in teaching and learning in higher, further and continuing education, distilling out as it does practical guidelines for closer communication between teacher and student.

As before my thanks are due to the McGraw-Hill Book Company for permission to quote a passage from J.A. Peddiwell, *The Sabre-tooth Curriculum*, New York, 1939; to Pan Books Ltd., for permission to quote from my book *Study to Succeed* (1973), p. 61; and to Tetradon Publications Ltd., for permission to quote from *Effective Learning: a practical guide for students*.

I should also like to give acknowledgement to the source of the communication skills bibliography. It is an updated and select version of a listing which originally appeared as a result of a review undertaken while at the University of Surrey and produced for limited circulation as *Communication Skills: results of a survey of books, materials and courses in universities, polytechnics and institutes of higher education in the United Kingdom*, by P.J. Hills, P.F. Gardiner and P.J. McVey (July 1979).

My thanks are also due to the many colleagues and friends, teachers and students who have commented on, or who have been exposed to, the various parts of the text. Thanks also to my wife for her patience, forbearance and hard work in the preparation of the text.

P.J. Hills
Cambridge

1 ON HUMAN COMMUNICATION

In 1957 Professor Colin Cherry wrote *On Human Communication*. He wrote it to give 'some notion of the relations between the diverse studies of communication, of the causes and the growth of this modern interest'. In the preface to the third edition (1977) he wrote:

> The book was first written as an attempt to make a case for the study of human communication as an academic subject. That case still stands, though the nature of such a study is still far from crystal clear.

It was Cherry's book which inspired the first edition of this book *Teaching and Learning as a Communication Process* (Croom Helm, London, 1979). The word 'communication' comes from the Latin 'communicare' meaning 'to share', and, as I had outlined in a previous book *The Self-Teaching Process in Higher Education* (Hills, 1976), I see the act of teaching and of learning as an act of sharing.

Essentially this book looks at the process of educational communication as an interaction between individuals transmitting the standards, values and skills of a society. This interaction has been vastly extended and refined by twentieth century man, who is using a wide variety of techniques and devices both to communicate knowledge of culture and heritage, to influence others, and to store, process and retrieve the results of this communication.

Education As a Communication Process

Education can be seen as a communication process between society and the individual; and we need constantly to keep this in mind when looking at the relevance of our formal system of education. Education must be looked at constantly in order to determine how well it is communicating the standards of society and the store of man's knowledge.

My favourite story in this respect is the cautionary tale told by Peddiwell in *The Sabre-tooth Curriculum* (Peddiwell, 1939). This story tells of a prehistoric tribe which decided to introduce education to its children in the form of teaching skills designed to meet particular survival needs. The first subject in the curriculum was 'fish-grabbing-with-the-bare hands', ensuring more and better food by catching fish from the streams and pools of clear water near where the tribe lived. The second subject was 'woolly-horse-clubbing'. The woolly horses came down to the water to drink and graze in a nearby meadow. Their coats provided skins to keep the tribe warm. The third subject was 'sabre-tooth-tiger-scaring-with-fire' using firebrands to keep the tigers away from the water and give the tribe greater security.

In the course of time a new ice age came to that part of the world and a glacier came down from a nearby mountain range. When it came close to the stream which ran through the tribe's valley it began to melt into the stream. The dirt and gravel that the glacier had collected on its long journey dropped into the water, so that it became muddy. Since all the slow-moving fish had been caught by the tribe with their bare hands, only the quick-moving fish were left and these were easily able to hide under boulders thrown into the stream by the glacier and dart swiftly and unseen through the muddy water. So no matter how good a man's fish-grabbing education had been, he could not grab fish if there were no fish to grab.

The other subjects in the curriculum, horse-clubbing and tiger-scaring, became equally irrelevant as the nature of the land near the glacier changed. The woolly horses died out and the tigers went away, but their place was taken by agile antelopes and ferocious bears. Skills of fish-net-making, antelope-snare-construction and bear-catching were developed. But, meanwhile, as you have probably guessed, what was still being taught back in the schools was 'fish-grabbing, woolly-horse-clubbing and tiger-scaring'. The teachers in the prehistoric schools were no longer in touch with the needs of their tribe.

The cautionary tale is, of course, that in the fast changing world of today, relevance is of greater importance than it has ever been.

There is a great need to ensure that the content and type of our courses in schools and in institutions of higher, further and continuing education are subject to regular review.

Educational Communication: A Historical Context

As the needs and standards of society change from age to age, so the problems of communication repeat themselves again and again in the context of education. The purpose of education in Ancient Greece was to safeguard society through concentrating on education in two main areas: the attainment of physical fitness and the preservation of religious and moral standards. Well into the fifth century BC the educational ideal of Athens was the soldier-citizen. After the Persian Wars Athens became not just a warrior state, but a thriving industrial and commercial business centre. This had a great effect on its ideas of education. An educational system grew up which combined areas of religion, intellect and aestheticism. Greek education communicated its standards to its citizens by interactive methods. The methods advocated by Socrates in the middle of the third century BC provide one illustration of this idea of interaction. The Socratic method of instruction was carried out in the form of a guided set of questions and answers through which the teacher sought to lead the student to knowledge and conclusions.

Socrates' intention was to stimulate thought in his 'pupils'. He often pretended ignorance of a point and let his pupil 'teach' him. The whole idea was stemmed from the Greek desire for fluency of speech; out of this need rose the Sophists who travelled the country lecturing on rhetoric. Socrates, influenced by their teaching, took up the challenge and consequently became the most famous teacher in Greece through his dialogue. His aim was to guide students through various processes of thought to an awareness of truth discovered by themselves. This he did by question and answer and by examples which he gave to his pupils; in fact he taught by an inductive method.

Time and time again throughout history, as theories and practice of education developed, we see emphasis on 'self' and the fact that our own senses are there to be used. Comenius in the seventeenth century believed in the absolute necessity of having a 'right way of teaching', in order to give a good grounding in knowledge upon which 'self' development might build. He, like Socrates before him, saw the teacher as the 'centre'. He conceived the idea of a universal education. Education as he saw it was the most complete preparation possible for life. It could only be effective if account was taken of the learner, and therefore instruction had to be fitted to the learner, not the other way round. One could say that in him was the beginning of modern education.

Rousseau (1712–1778), in the eighteenth century, continued the trend towards the modern idea of education as did others in his era. He, too, advocated the need for national education; without it there would be no means of making good citizens. It could not be imposed upon them, he believed; the original nature of each child had to be developed. Rousseau believed that, to achieve this, education must be 'solitary', 'rationalist' and 'utilitarian'. His scheme for education was derived from his principle of age-grouping. His main writing on education was in *Emile*, the story of a boy growing up. This had an immediate effect in the eighteenth century, people began to adopt his ideas and, what was most important, to realise how fundamental education was to the building of society. They became aware of the necessity of considering new schemes which might improve the educational process.

One might think that the great influence of Rousseau's theories would have smothered the idea of individual development, concerned as he was with the idea of making good citizens. This, however, was not true as we see when we consider people such as Pestalozzi (1746–1827). He, like Rousseau, believed that for the best education good parents and a good home were essential, and that the family was the best example a school could follow. Unlike Rousseau, Pestalozzi realised the status of the home was not so important, it was the example set by it that mattered, i.e. the example of the parents. When, in educational establishments, teachers were set in the position of parents at home, that is, as the centre piece and example, the development of the individual was possible. The teacher was the instrument by which the ideals and ideas were communicated. From this position he was led to a whole scheme of education.

Each step in the education of an individual must be within the reach of his intellect. The chief weakness in Pestalozzi's system was that he failed to recognise that method had to change for a pupil as he developed. He never considered methods which might be best for those who had mastered the basic elements. This was left to those who followed in an age when the world began a change which is still going on. Many people, however, consider Pestalozzi to be the founder of the elementary system of education.

The idea of producing 'good men' was the fundamental principle behind education according to Herbart (1776–1834) who stated a belief in Pestalozzi's methods, though he carried them further. His basic concept was that through knowledge comes morality and towards this end his ideas were directed. Interest, according to him, was an important factor in the learning process; the student's mind must become absorbed in whatever he was learning. For a teacher to be boring or a student bored hindered the whole process of communication from teacher to student: 'interest means self-activity'. Here we have reference to the self-teaching process which is of such interest to us in the second half of the twentieth century. Herbart is noteworthy for his idea of four stages in instruction: clearness, association, system and method. Today these four stages have been developed into five by his advocates: preparation, presentation, association, condensation and application, all of which may readily be applied to the educational communication process.

The first half of the nineteenth century saw many idealist educators who believed that good communication was essential in the education process. Froebel, though remembered for his ideas on the education of the very young, had a fundamental concept which can be applied to the whole range of educational progress, that of systematic activity.

The experiments, so prevalent in the nineteenth century, to discover the best system of universal education, have continued into the twentieth century, and many educators, such as Maria Montessori, established experimental schools. All stress the idea of individual development, that the individual is the important element in the teaching/learning process.

Educational Communication

I have touched on only a few of the outstanding educators of the past, those particularly concerned with educational communication used to enhance the individual and advance learning both for its own sake and for that of the world, endeavouring to create a better man through self-directed education. We shall find traces of these concepts in the chapters which follow.

This book concentrates on educational communication, on how teachers and students act and interact. However, with the increased use of computers and the increasing possibilities in telecommunication networks for data transmission, it is necessary to begin to address fundamental questions on how society and formal education, as it exists today, will begin to change in the coming years. With the help of a small group of contributors I began to question this in the December 1984 issue of *Science and Public Policy* under the theme 'Human Communication in an Age of Electronic Revolution' (Hills, 1984); this theme is continued in Chapter 10.

2 EDUCATION AS A COMMUNICATION PROCESS

The communications model of Shannon and Weaver (1949), originally applied to the development of electrical systems, can be and has been successfully applied to human communication (for example see Berlo, 1960). The model consists essentially of the following linked parts:

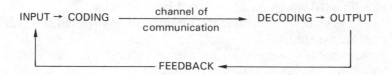

Let us examine this model in terms of educational communication.

Input

The input in educational communication can be thought of as society transmitting its knowledge, skills, values and standards to coming generations. The teacher supplies and manages the 'input'. In the case of school subjects input is often accepted as the subject matter of a particular specialisation, largely pre-determined by an examination syllabus. This is a very limited view of the input, since teachers bring to the situation their own attitudes to the subject, to life and society in general, all of which are also likely to be transmitted to the students.

Coding

Coding takes place when teachers put facts, statements, ideas, attitudes etc. in the sort of form which students can assimilate and thus learn from. Considering this in broad terms, messages are coded into the printed word, visual images or sound. These are modified, changed and reinforced by a variety of non-verbal messages. Coding is thus the process of making the desired input visible to the student; and therefore teachers have the responsibility of seeing that the coding is such that the student is able both to receive the material and to understand and decode it.

Teachers make their ideas visible by coding them into a series of symbols which go to make up spoken or written language or pictures. The essential condition is that the student should speak and understand the same series of symbols, including the specialised symbols associated with particular subjects. There are essential questions which ought to be asked here such as:

Does the student understand the meaning of any specialist words used in the subject?

Is the student's background knowledge sufficient for the level at which the teacher is coding the subject?

Without the compatibility of coding and decoding processes there will be no communication, since symbols can only be representations of events and not the events themselves.

Channel of Communication

This should convey the message to the student accurately. If a teacher is directly concerned, he may be using his voice as the channel of communication in conjunction with a variety of visual methods, the simplest of which is the chalk-board. I still remember vividly the method of one of my mathematics lecturers, who used to talk at the blackboard while he wrote his notes on it. As he wrote the notes with one hand he shielded them from view with his body and rubbed them out with the other hand. His channels of communication hardly ever reached the students.

There are now available many varieties of audio-visual equipment which can be used either to aid the teacher or as a method of instruction without the teacher in group or individual work by students. On the visual side these range from simple aids like the overhead projector and 35mm slide-projector, to ciné-projectors, video-recorders, video-disc players and computers. On the audio side the most versatile piece of equipment is still the audio-cassette recorder which can be used in conjunction with many other forms of visual display. It is often found most useful when used in conjunction with simple printed materials. When considering channels of communication apart from the voice, one must not neglect the printed page. This has many possibilities for presenting textual and diagrammatic materials, both as teacher support material and when designed for individual use as worksheets, programmed material or used with audio-taped material.

The main consideration in choosing the channel of communication is that it should clearly and accurately convey the message to the student. The point previously mentioned, i.e. that symbols are only representations of events and not the events themselves, should be stressed again here. Therefore, the message conveyed by the chosen channel of communication can in no way convey the same message which the actual event would convey. The message conveyed, in addition to being compounded of the choice of symbols selected by the teacher and the way in which they are received by the student, has certain inherent characteristics which are present as a necessary part of the channel of communication chosen. This is well illustrated in the following way: consider a subject viewed by projecting an image of it using a high-definition 35mm colour slide and compare that with one of it viewed in a relatively low-definition television picture of the same size. You would find the limiting characteristics of the latter strikingly apparent.

Noise

In the original communication model, noise in the system was the sort of thing which renders a telephone conversation unclear or produces crackles on the line, masking the speech. The necessity for clarity and accuracy of message has already been stressed, but in teaching and learning there are many sources of noise which can mask or obscure the message, whatever channel of communication is being used.

One quite considerable source of noise is the teaching environment itself. There is still too little attention paid to the large variety of factors which go to make up the teaching environment. Often, the main requirement seems to be that it is a room containing a sufficient number of chairs, and that it has a blackboard or facility for an overhead projector. Qualities of comfort of the chairs, visual impact of the colour of the walls and floor covering, sound quality and spatial dimensions of the walls seem to be ignored. All these and more are important if one is considering potential noise in the system. The size of a group also directly influences the physical noise, since the larger the group the more likely are the members of it to produce noises like sneezes and coughs, chair moving etc. Someone sitting at the back of such a group could have a considerable degree of interference with their reception of the message.

The biggest potential source of noise in face-to-face teaching is the teacher. Concerned with getting communication across to students the teacher must be clear in his purpose, making sure that the material is as clear and as unambiguous as possible. Appropriate channels of communication must be chosen, using a variety of techniques to ensure that students receive and learn the material presented.

Decoding and Output

The 'output' received by the student is not always that intended by the designers of the 'input'. What is received will depend on a number of factors, including the student's previous knowledge of a subject. Teachers expect students coming from school to an institution of higher education to have a sufficient background in a subject to be able to decode the material presented. Students are also often expected to possess skills of notetaking, writing up practical work, an ability to use books and extract information from them, and to have acquired skills of argument and discussion. This is so often obviously not the case.

First, the possession of a recognised qualification in a subject at school level is no guarantee that sufficient background to a subject is possessed. Part of a teacher's task when a student enters a course of instruction should be to determine whether the student does possess sufficient background knowledge and, if he does not, to help him to acquire it. As for skills of notetaking, writing up etc., these also cannot be assumed, and teachers would do well to discuss these points with their students, providing help where necessary. These points are taken up again in later chapters.

Feedback

The student is central to the communication process which in the formal educational setting includes teachers, books, audio-visual media and a range of resource materials and information sources. 'Channels of communication' are for the most part those of sight and sound and should be arranged to convey the input to the student in as accurate a way as possible. 'Feedback' plays an essential part in regulating this. Feedback is an important part of any self-regulating system, e.g. the thermostat on an electric radiator feeds back information to the system on the surrounding temperature and thus the supply of electricity to the radiator is regulated to keep the surrounding air at a constant temperature. Human beings are largely self-regulating mechanisms, for example, they shiver or perspire to maintain their body temperature against extremes of outside temperature.

Feedback from student to teacher giving information on how the message has been received is an essential part of the educational communication process. Such feedback enables the teacher to vary the input depending on student response and so reduce or eliminate errors of decoding or factors caused by 'noise' in the system.

Teacher/Student Processes

For the purposes of the chapters which follow the model of educational communication can be simplified to the following elements:

```
                      channel of communication
   TEACHER        ————————————————————————————>        STUDENT
                    <————————————————————————
                         feedback channel
```

Feedback is included in its various aspects within each chapter.

Although in the following account there is inevitably overlapping between the categories, chapters dealing with teacher and student processes are as follows:

Teacher Processes and Channels of Communication

Chapter 3   The Teacher as Manager of the Learning Process
Chapter 4   The Psychology of Educational Communication
Chapter 5   Interpersonal and Group Processes
Chapter 6   Verbal and Non-Verbal Communication
Chapter 7   Audio-Visual Communication

Student Processes

Chapter 8   The Student as Receiver
Chapter 9   The Student as Communicator
Chapter 10   Teaching, Learning and Communication considers the educational process in the light of our changing society.

3 THE TEACHER AS MANAGER OF THE LEARNING PROCESS

If teaching were merely a matter of communicating the content of a course to a student without worrying too much about what happens at the student end, then the taught lesson or lecture might be considered to be an ideal and efficient way of doing this. The teacher stands up in front of a large group of students and communicates for an uninterrupted period of some thirty to fifty minutes. This exposes the material to the student and gets through the syllabus reasonably quickly. It is administratively convenient since a large number of students can be 'processed' by one teacher in one room. However, the educational communication process should not be for the convenience of the teacher: it should be for the benefit of the student.

Fleming sees the teacher as a 'student of motivation . . . a promoter of learning . . . an observer of growth . . . craftsman and technician . . . administrator and therapist'. (Fleming, 1968). The teacher exists to help the student to perceive the communication as clearly as possible and should, therefore, be concerned with every aspect of the total educational environment in which the student exists and works. There are now many ways in which the student can acquire information and learn facts, concepts, skills etc. These consist of either interacting with the teacher, or by using a variety of independent study methods, using video-tape, simulations and programmes on a micro-computer, accessing computer data-bases etc. The role of the teacher has thus moved even farther from one of 'disseminator of all knowledge' towards one of 'manager of the learning process'. The teacher's role embraces all the facets of a student's development which are reflected in the list which follows.

The teacher needs to:

1. Think about course work both in terms of academic content and the needs of the student.
2. Find out if a student is in a position to be able to receive

and understand the material of a course and, if not, to help him.

3. Determine if a student has the necessary skills to cope with his courses, e.g. notetaking, writing up, skills of discussion and argument and, if not, to help him to acquire them.
4. Take account of the student's level of growth and physical and intellectual ability.
5. Arouse the student's interest in the subject material and help him to maintain that interest.
6. Keep the student aware of his progress.
7. Be more open about course work and requirements, especially if self-teaching methods are to be used.
8. Talk informally to students, revealing rather than concealing his own ideas and problems.
9. Take care not to overestimate the amount the students know.
10. Be aware of factors in interpersonal and group processes.
11. Be aware of the non-verbal content of his communications.

These are in addition to the more mechanistic or administrative tasks of providing and supporting the actual learning materials and equipment. This latter will not be developed in detail here, but for an account of the organisation and management of support services in further and higher education see *The Organisation and Management of Educational Technology* (Tucker, 1979).

The concept of educational technology is the key to the changing role of the teacher. In November 1964, B.F. Skinner gave a lecture to the Royal Society entitled 'The Technology of Teaching' (Skinner, 1968). This was perhaps the forerunner of the term 'Educational Technology' with its implication that education is merely a mechanistic process. Indeed the programmed learning movement of the 1960s began to open up interactive aspects of the teaching/learning process which had previously been little explored. In June 1962 I wrote enthusiastically in the *School Science Review*:

There are many questions as yet unanswered, but whatever the outcome of present researches it is certain that the programmed learning method is an extremely efficient method of teaching. In industry for imparting practical skills it may become invaluable. In schools and science laboratories it may free the teacher from routine learning processes and enable him to concentrate on those things which a tight examination usually excludes. (Hills, 1962)

At that time I firmly believed that better and more structured programmes gave the answer to the need for more effective learning. I, like many others, was concentrating entirely on passing knowledge embodied in a series of subject courses to the student. The principles of active learning, small units of material proceeding from the simple to the complex, could be proved to have worked from the results of tests given to students immediately after they had completed the programmed material. What became apparent was that the programmes, although they were passing information, when taken *en masse*, were producing effects of boredom and strain by overloading the student with long sequences of textual material unrelieved by any other methods.

In the 1960s the situation was complicated by the over-commercialisation of the process. The number of 'teaching machines' designed to display programmed learning sequences multiplied at a tremendous rate only to come to a rapid and untimely end, because manufacturers were unable or unwilling to ensure a sufficient supply of programmes, in a variety of subjects, to go with their machines. *The Yearbook of the Association for Programmed Learning and Educational Technology 1974/5* illustrated this with the following commmment:

Between 1969 and 1971 the number of machines . . . available sank from 30 to 18 . . . the number of new programmes available for teaching machines is quite small. (Howe and Romiszowski, 1974)

In the Year Book for 1966/7 only six actual teaching machines are listed (Howe and Romiszowski, 1976). Because of the unfortunate consequences of over-commercialisation of the subject, the programmed learning movement was thought to be dead; in practice it has only changed and adapted. The movement reflected the character of the sixties, a time of change and thought, a time when in a number of fields there was a growing awareness of the student as an individual. It is true that many of the programmed learning sequences of that time were boring and repetitive, but they emphasised the role of the student as learner and made at least some attempt to cater for the needs of the individual students with different levels of understanding and background.

The advent of the micro-computer has given this a new dimension as it is potentially a very flexible teaching/learning device which can provide much more than just the programmed sequences of the 1960s. It can be used for information retrieval, problem solving, the manipulation of mathematical models, simulation of a large number of situations, etc.

However, although the new patterns of learning and the methods which are emerging show effective ways of presenting course material and ensuring that students learn, one must never lose sight of the interactive human element in the teaching/learning process. This can be regarded as a mere counter-weight to the mechanistic aspects of some of the methods that are being developed such as computer assisted learning, or it can be regarded as a more fundamental aspect of the process of education for the transmission of the standards of our society. However one regards it, this interactive element is of vital importance.

If we examine again the list given above we find that it breaks down into two main areas of teacher action, namely:

1. Managing the process of education.
2. Ensuring a fuller and closer communication with the student.

Let us look at these two areas in more detail.

Managing the Process of Education

I have argued in *The Self-Teaching Process in Higher Education* (Hills, 1976) that it is important to help a student to learn not only while he is engaged in formal course work, but also to help him to become a self-directing individual. Mountford (1966) expresses the essence of this when he says that we need to:

provide the student with a body of positive knowledge which enhances his store of learning and in part equips him for his career in later life . . . To the limits of his capacity he is trained to collect evidence for himself and form a balanced judgement about it. He fortifies his ability to think for himself.

Whatever techniques have to be developed in order that the student should achieve these aims depends ultimately on the individual student himself, and it is the task of the teacher to help with this. Gilbert Highet's three principles of teaching still hold true today:

The first is clarity. Whatever you are teaching, make it clear. Make it as firm and as bright as sunlight. Not to yourself — that is easy. Make it clear to the people you are teaching — that is difficult.
The second is patience. Anything worth learning takes time to learn and time to teach.
The third principle is responsibility. It is a serious thing to interfere with another man's life. It is hard enough to guide one's own. (Highet, 1951)

Teachers can sometimes forget that with the increased number of methods, resources and techniques at their disposal they need to consider even more the needs of the student. This extends to more than just being ready to see and talk to students. They need a real appreciation of the way in which students view teachers. Parlett expressed this in terms of the student who sees the process as 'an educational contract that exists between someone who has knowledge and someone who does not' (Parlett *et al.*, 1976). Because most teachers are always ready to see and talk to students, they do not consider it a problem. Students, however, see a very real barrier. The reason often given for not speaking out in a group discussion is that students are afraid of voicing their opinions lest they appear foolish. They do not want teachers to know that they have problems because this may draw the teacher's attention to the fact that they are not doing very well. Although the barrier is a psychological one and is in the mind of the student, teachers, by omission, often do little to help. Just saying 'If you need any help, let me know' is not really enough. Teachers need to go out of their way to get to know students on the course, to be able to talk informally to them and, almost without them knowing, to assess whether they are in need of help and guidance.

Some indications of this were given in a review I carried out on student and teacher perceptions of the communication between one another:

> Students and teachers see a need for teachers to be tolerant, patient, relaxed, friendly, approachable, they should also be interested in students . . . be available and willing to help when wanted . . . Both parties expressed a wish to get to know each other outside teaching hours . . . perhaps both parties recognise the present lack of communication between them and are seeking ways of overcoming this. (Hills, 1976)

This survey of students' and teachers' expressed perceptions of course needs indicated the need for more informal communication between both parties. It has changed little today. This is an area which has in part contributed to the barrier between teachers and students simply because contact was limited to formal teaching only. This need not be so if the teacher can adopt a more open approach to the student, revealing rather than concealing his own ideas and the problems associated with course work. The teacher must attempt to meet and talk to students in a more informal way. This leads us to the second basic area.

Ensuring a Fuller and Closer Communication with the Student

Specific areas will be taken up in more detail in Chapter 8. Here let us explore this in terms of inputs to the student. These are:

(i) From the teacher in charge of the course giving information about the timetable, the syllabus, various administrative arrangements etc. There is a need to give students as much information as possible to help to orientate them to their new environment and the requirements of the course.

(ii) Course content in the form of a series of lectures supplemented by group discussions etc. The administrative convenience of the lesson or lecture has already been mentioned, but what has not been mentioned is that students and teachers appear to like them. Teachers like lectures because it gives them a sense of involvement with their students. It may be that teachers like the element of performance in this act of communication with a large group. Students sometimes behave as if the lecture is the only real part of the education process and that they gain knowledge by some sort of osmosis from sitting in lectures. In fact, the lecture can only display information to the student, it cannot ensure that he learns it. If a teacher has to give a series of lectures, the basic requirement is that he should put the information across clearly and distinctly. Handout notes giving the main structure of each lecture can help, as can some advice on taking notes from a lecture early in the course.

Since each teacher has his own style, it is particularly appropriate that he should talk a little to the students on how to take notes from lectures, since only he is likely to know his own style and preferences. One useful way of introducing this topic is to ask students to take outline notes during the first lecture of a series and allow time at the end for the lecturer to hand out his own version of the lecture notes. These can act as a basis for discussion and help to orientate the student's notetaking for the rest of the series.

(iii) From the teacher and other students in discussion groups and other forms of group work. Chapter 5 is particularly concerned with this area, and guidance on the advantages and methods of group work are given there. Teachers should bear in mind particularly that group work is most valuable as a means of encouraging discussion between students, so that they can share their ideas with others.

(iv) Directed reading for the student from the teacher. This is particularly important as it is all too easy to swamp a student by giving him a large reading list and expecting him to apply himself to reading. This is sometimes done without later making any reference to the material or finding out if the student has read it. The aim of a reading list, certainly at the beginning of a course, should be that the student

(a) realises that the teacher giving the course is for the most part only representing one viewpoint and that there are others
(b) is directed into a situation where he has to use the library

as part of his course
(c) becomes accustomed to using books and extracting information from them.

Such a reading list therefore should be carefully prepared so that
it is relatively short and directed perhaps to specific sections or
pages in a book (not simply the whole book). The material should
be integrated with course material and not be an optional extra.
A further elementary point, but one which will make the librarian
very happy, is to ensure that the material on the reading list is
in the library before the course begins. In later years of a course
the purpose of a reading list can change and become much more
non-directive as the student gains in confidence and ability.

(v) Information from the teacher to the student on his performance on a piece of practical work, an essay or other assignment
which he has completed. This is concerned with feedback on the
outputs from the student and is dealt with under the next heading.

(vi) Information received by the student on his performance in
tests or term examinations. Examinations and tests are normally
thought of as tools of assessment, which they are, but they can
be used to help the student to consolidate the course work, to inform him of the progress he is making on the course and to provide him with practice in examination technique. If these latter
purposes are intended, then it is essential that the teachers should
mark the tests or examinations and return them to the student as
quickly as possible for maximum benefit. If the tests are to help
the student, there is no reason why they should not be self-marked
tests. Self-tests of this kind have been described in use with a first-
year electrical engineering course consisting of:

(a) a pre-knowledge test, designed to show the student what
he should know upon entry to the course, and
(b) tests given at pre-determined intervals. The latter tests were
designed to test the material content of the course.
After completing a test, the student was given an answer sheet
which enabled him to mark his own answers. Thus he was able
to see immediately in which areas his knowledge might be weak.
(Hills, 1976)

For a useful account of the purposes of assessment, the ways in which it can be used as an aid to student learning and as a technique for monitoring student progress see *Assessing Students, Appraising Teaching* (Clift and Imrie, 1981).

(vii) Informal inputs from other students. Inputs of this kind can be helpful when a student experiences the kind of 'psychological barrier' previously mentioned. It is sometimes difficult for a teacher to appreciate the confusion or lack of comprehension experienced by a student, since the explanation given to the students is obviously quite clear to the teacher. This is where other students who have understood a problem are in a much better position to help than the teacher, because they are working mostly in the same frame of reference as the bewildered student. This point may not necessarily occur to students seeking help, and it does no harm for the teacher to point this out. He might also point out the advantages of an informal group of students working together.

(viii) Reading done by the student. If a student does get as far as admitting to a teacher that he has gaps in his background knowledge, he or she can be given a good introductory text to read. However, it should be borne in mind that what may seem to be a good introductory text to the teacher may not appear so to the student. All too often the gap between the elementary text and the more advanced work of the course appears unbridgeable and it may be wise for the teacher to arrange informal discussions with the student to see how he or she is coping with the work. The teacher should also remember that the student with problems of background knowledge may not come to him; therefore a general point made to all students on the helpfulness of a good introductory text will not come amiss.

(ix) Non-verbal information given largely unconsciously by the teacher. This will be dealt with in Chapter 6. It is important that the teacher is at least aware of this channel of communication and makes some attempt to bring it under control, because it is mainly this non-verbal information that tells the student about the teacher's attitude to the work. It also tells him what emphasis the teacher puts on different parts of the course.

Those interested in exploring this further should look at *Educational Staff Development* (Main, 1985). He proposes a model of staff development with the teacher as a learner offering him or her the kind of support we have been discussing above. The model described has already been successful in a number of sectors of education and in several countries.

4 THE PSYCHOLOGY OF EDUCATIONAL COMMUNICATION

In the teaching and learning process, communication between a teacher and a student is concerned with the transmission of a message either to increase a student's knowledge or to change his attitudes, his beliefs or his behaviour in some way.

Learning can be defined as a process of acquiring knowledge or changing attitudes, behaviour or beliefs by contact with external events. The purpose of formulating learning theories is to give a deeper understanding of the process of learning, but whereas in the past psychologists based their consideration of the communication which must exist between the teacher and the learner in terms of stimulus and response without regard to the human organisms involved, recent interest has centred more on the individual and the variety of motives, stimulations and functions which modify his reception of the message.

In this chapter we shall explore briefly theories of learning which are concerned with stimulus/response interactions, principally the work of Watson, Thorndyke and Skinner. We shall then discuss work concerned with the student as an active processor of information and consider what practical principles of learning can be applied in order to help in the design of course materials.

Stimulus/Response Theories

In 1913 John Watson (1878–1958) published a paper, 'Psychology as the Behaviourist Views It'. As the father of the behaviourist movement, Watson was not interested in the inner self of the person but only in the way in which thought and emotion showed itself in behaviour. He was concerned with reducing complex behaviour to simpler stimulus/response units so that any learning which occurred at the level of these simple units could then be built into complex repertoires of behaviour.

As an extension of this he was also concerned with the principles of 'frequency' and 'recency'. That the more often we make a given response to a given stimulus the more likely we are to make that response again is the notion which lies behind the 'frequency' principle. The principle of 'recency' is that the more recently we have made a particular response to a stimulus the more likely we are to make that response again. Although Watson's ideas were never carried through to reach clear explanations, he made a contribution to psychology in his emphasis on the study of observable behaviour, thus paving the way for later behaviourism.

Edward Thorndyke (1874–1949) based his view of learning not simply on the strengthening effect of the stimulus and response occurring together but more on the effects following the response. He formulated the 'law of effect' which states that strengthening of the stimulus/response bonds occurs when followed by satisfying conditions, i.e. something in the nature of reinforcement by reward for good behaviour.

The Importance of Reinforcement

B.F. Skinner (b. 1904) has long been concerned specifically with reinforcement as a basic factor in learning. With regard to Watson's principles of 'frequency' and 'recency', which he considers as the theory of 'learning by doing', he proposes that rather than learning occurring by the principle of 'frequency' as defined above, it is the frequent drill practice that enables our students to remember a particular response. The principle of 'recency' he considers occurs under favourable conditions, i.e. the conditions reinforce the response. He reduces traditional ways of characterising teaching and learning to learning by doing, learning from experience, learning by trial and error. He dismisses these theories in the following words: 'such theories are now of historical interest only . . . We may turn instead to a more adequate analysis of the changes which take place as a student learns.' (Skinner, 1968).

Skinner's 'more adequate analysis' is concerned with what he refers to as 'operant behaviour'. He suggests that whereas certain behaviour is elicited by specific stimuli, 'operant behaviour' is emitted by the organism itself. He considers that most behaviour is of this kind, e.g. talking, eating, walking etc. His concern is thus not with the stimulus/response connections but with the ways in which 'operant behaviour' could be brought under control and subject to modification.

Skinner's best known article which has a special bearing on teaching and learning as communication is 'The Science of Learning and the Art of Teaching', first read at a conference at the University of Pittsburgh in March 1954. In it he describes briefly his work on the shaping of the behaviour of pigeons and goes on to apply his ideas to the teaching and learning process with students. He is particularly critical of the relative infrequency and delay in reinforcement of material presented to and produced by students. This article describes primarily the programme of work pursued at Harvard under his guidance. The results of this work are reported in his article 'Teaching Machines' (Skinner, 1958).

In this article he defines the teaching situation as follows: 'A student is "taught" in the sense that he is induced to engage in new forms of behaviour.' He mentions that in order to do this there has to be some form of 'teaching machine', thus producing a situation akin to that of having a private tutor who insists on material being understood before the student is allowed to move on, thus enabling the student to work at his own pace.

The communication of information by what was basically a linear question and answer sequence became part of the programmed learning movement. Although there were a number of other names and a variety of intricacies associated with the programmed learning of the 1960s, we shall not pursue them here. Leith's booklet *Second Thoughts on Programmed Learning* (Leith, 1969), should prove useful for anyone wishing to take this further. For our purpose the importance of the programmed learning movement lies in the practical principles for learning which emerged from the work of Skinner and others. These were concerned with motivation, activity, reinforcement, and limits on the amount and complexity of material presented etc. These practical learning principles will be taken up again later in this chapter.

So far we have been concerned with learning theories which consider that complex behaviour patterns are capable of being broken down into simple units where stimulus to the organism, response from the organism, and conditions under which these occur are the important variables. The use of the impersonal word 'organism' serves to show what little regard these learning theories had for the recipient of the stimulus and for the inner workings of the organism necessary to produce a response. The Gestalt psychologists attempted to redress this balance since they were concerned not simply with the mechanistic aspects of behaviour and the connections between them, but also with the way in which an organism interpreted and perceived stimuli presented to it as a unified whole.

Insightful Learning

The Gestalt movement (the German word 'gestalt' means 'form' or 'pattern') was started by the German psychologist Max Wertheimer (1880–1943). Whereas Gestalt psychologists concentrated mainly on the way in which the organism restructured the stimuli presented to it and this depended on the way in which they were perceived, Kurt Lewin (1890–1947) took this concept further. He was concerned with aspects of motivation, needs, personality, etc. Lewin's 'Field theory' of learning was concerned with how a learner gains insight into himself and the things around him, and how he then uses this to react to events around him. Perhaps the most important contribution made to the understanding of learning was the concept of 'insight'. Insightful learning occurs when one suddenly feels that one really understands or, as my mathematics teacher used to say, when 'the penny has finally dropped'.

Practical Learning Principles

With the increasing use of micro-computers for educational purposes, there is now considerable concern about the ways in which students process information. The Economic and Social Research Council's present research initiative in the area of micro-computers and cognitive learning processes has its roots in a report *Micro-*

computers in Education (Sage and Smith, 1983). In it, attention is drawn to the present lack of focus in this area by the UK Research Community. The authors argue that the fundamental need is for research which 'will inform the design and implementation of learning experiences based on the information technology applications in a variety of contexts'. They believe that such work will contribute to theoretical models which will assist the development of practical learning principles. It is true that very few general practical principles can be distilled from the variety of learning theories which exist at present, although the work of educational psychologists like Bruner, Rogers, Perry and Pask all reflect the present concern with the student not as a passive recipient of a communication, but as an active processor of information.

The book of readings *How Students Learn* (Entwistle and Hounsell, 1975) provides a summary of most current learning theories. A useful overview of theoretical approaches to learning appears in the book *Adult Learning* (Lovell, 1980). Although this is concerned with the differences between learning over the whole range of ages between sixteen and sixty, it has sections on the complex nature of learning, learning cognitive information, cognitive strategies and skill learning.

From an analysis of learning theories, although it is difficult to extract practical principles for learning, they all centre on the internal processes of the learner:

1. motivation of the learner
2. the physical and intellectual ability of the learner
3. the need for perception of meaningful relationships by the learner
4. the need for feedback on his progress
5. the experiencing of satisfactory personality adjustment and social growth by the learner.

These principles contain a mixture of factors, most of which are capable of being manipulated directly by the teacher in designing educational communications for students. Some, however, like maturation, can only be taken account of by the teacher; he has little or no direct control over them.

In this section I shall be concerned only with factors over which the teacher does have control and where the design of communications or the framework in which it is presented can affect the reception of the message. These factors can be expressed in terms of the following keywords: motivation, activity, understanding, and feedback. Let us consider each of these in turn.

Motivation

Motivation is concerned both with factors of arousal of interest and with maintenance of that interest. Since curiosity is thought to be a natural trait in human beings, interest should be aroused if some novel stimulus is presented; conversely interest will be diminished if a task becomes repetitive or boring. This is often the experience of a lecturer when his interest wanes in a subject because he has to give the same lecture time after time. If, however, the presentation can be varied or new material introduced, all the interest and enthusiasm for the subject revives.

Arousal of interest can be seen very clearly in young children because everything is a novel experience, and therefore new stimuli are constantly being presented. The experience of teachers in junior schools is that in many instances once a child's interest has been aroused the challenge of exploring a new situation can occupy the child for long periods, often for longer than an adult coming new to the same situation. This may be due to the adult's ability to relate a new situation to knowledge he already possesses, thus shortening the period of time necessary to absorb the new information. This is a point which we shall take up again below.

The need for the arousal of interest thus argues for the need to present material in a way that not only engages the student in the task but which also, most importantly, contains elements of challenge. Further, although the arousal of interest may be sufficient to ensure maintenance of interest in young children, something more is required for adults. Apart from the need to design the material so that it continues to engage the interest of adults, this interest should be maintained by the teacher. This can often be achieved by keeping a feeling of personal contact apparent. The results of the well-known Hawthorn experiment support this. An experiment comparing external incentives with the development of an *esprit de corps* in the workers was conducted at the Hawthorn works of the Western Electric Company. The general result of this experiment appeared to be that external incentives had less effect on the work than that produced by better morale and the feeling that the management had a personal interest in each worker.

The personal interest in a student is, or should be, a normal factor in a teacher's repertoire, but this is not necessarily so for a lecturer. This is perhaps due to both the freer atmosphere and the feeling that a lecturer is there only to lecture and to have little other contact with students. The two points which emerge most strongly for any teacher or lecturer at any level are the need to present material in such a way that will both engage and maintain a student's interest by making the material stimulating, and by making him feel that he is not being left to struggle with it completely on his own. The development and maintenance of group work and group feeling with other students can also contribute to this; this will be taken up again in Chapter 5.

Activity

The principle of activity is a fairly obvious one, for without some level of activity in the student, learning cannot take place. The picture of the lecture situation most commonly presented is that of the passive student and the active lecturer; the process should, however, be designed to turn towards inducing activity in the student. The need for activity was one of the central themes of the programmed learning movement where the assumption was that a good level of activity could be maintained by making the student work through material containing a sequence of questions and answers of increasing complexity. The problem was that these materials were restrictive, repetitive and often boring.

Present trends towards the individualisation of instruction as exemplified in the Postlethwaite Audio Tutorial approach, the Keller Plan and others (Hills, 1976) also build in these elements of activity by working with structured workbooks, practical work and a variety of media. What is most important with regard to activity, however, is the need to ensure that the student knows how to be active. Take, for example, the lecture situation described earlier. The fact that a student is, to all appearances, sitting passively in a lecture does not mean that his mind is not actively engaged by it. This problem will be of particular concern in Chapter 8 when we shall discuss the situation of the student as receiver. This chapter will look at the process in terms of how a student can actively deal with a number of inputs presented to him. In the case of the lecture the need for activity is stressed in terms of the difference between merely 'hearing' and 'actively listening' — a notetaking and questioning process is advocated. Chapter 8 also looks in detail at the processes within the student and the levels and types of activity he needs to undertake.

Understanding

From the moment a child is born he begins to acquire information, to form concepts and ideas about the the world in which he lives. At first these will be limited to his immediate environment, but as his life expands he begins to learn things about his neighbourhood, his town, his country. Each of us has built up a complex set of understandings about many things. These we can call 'frames of reference' as they are our internal models of the world about us. Whenever new information is presented to us we try to fit it into our existing understanding of things, to make it consistent with the frames of reference which we already hold. There is a tendency in terms of this to minimise inconsistencies between what we already know and what is presented to us. Read again the first sentence of this section — you may have already seen that the word 'the' appears twice in the first sentence, but then again you may not have noticed this. Our daily newspapers are full of this type of inconsistency, often because of faulty proof reading, but it is something we tend not to notice. Some householders use the tendency we have of minimising inconsistencies by putting up a notice outside their garage door which reads 'Polite notice. No parking'. Usually, when someone sees this for the first time he misreads 'polite' as 'police', thus giving the notice more authority than it might otherwise have.

When a young child has new information or a new experience presented to him it can alter his behaviour drastically. However, this does not usually occur to such a great extent in adults, since a frame of reference already exists into which the new information is incorporated. It is important for us as teachers to recognise that when we communicate new information to our students we should attempt to ensure that each student receiving it has a sufficient understanding of the background and context of the communication.

Feedback

Just as we should ensure that a student has a background knowledge of a subject before he goes further into it, so we ought to help him to continue to monitor his progress, giving him continued assurance that he is progressing or alternatively giving him help if he is failing to achieve his objectives. Bugelski expresses this as: 'Learning goes forward with relatively greater effectiveness when the learner is provided with some criterion for indicating specifically what progress he is making'. (Bugelski, 1956)

This statement, made some fifty years ago, is still somewhat at variance with the way in which students are given information on the results of tests, by the comments and marks on an essay, and by end-of-term and end-of-year examinations. In these 'traditional' ways or providing feedback to students on their progress there is often a considerable delay in, for example, marking an essay and returning it to the student. The point is that essays, tests, and examinations have been thought of as tools of assessment for the teacher in order that he may see how the student is getting on, not for the student to monitor his own progress.

The possibility of feedback of information to the student on his progress is becoming increasingly recognised as individualised methods like the Keller Plan begin to be more widely known. In the Keller Plan the course is split up into units of material each of which contains a test of progress which the student takes at the end. The test is then marked by a tutor and discussed with the student immediately so that any problems can be sorted out. The idea of feedback need not however be confined to individualised methods of education. It can and should be applied to all methods. In *The Self-Teaching Process in Higher Education* (Hills, 1976), work is described incorporating feedback which uses self-test questions as a support system to what was mainly a conventional first-year university course consisting of a series of lectures. Work with a first-year course on chemical bonding which used booklets of basic information containing self-test questions for feedback with lectures given mainly as problem-solving sessions is also described. These and other ways of keeping students informed of their progress are perfectly possible within the framework of any type of course; they also carry the great advantage that the student has closer contact with the teacher. This helps to maintain motivation.

As more work is done on the ways in which students process information we shall begin to perceive how to structure and present material effectively to individual students. This represents a swing of concern in the communication process from the teacher presenting material with little idea of how it is received by the student to a realisation that in learning it is the individual student who is important. In the absence of more definitive guidelines teachers should design their courses and subject material bearing in mind that motivation, activity, understanding and feedback, as described here, are all important principles to help the student in his reception of the educational message.

5 INTERPERSONAL AND GROUP PROCESSES

Interpersonal Processes

A teacher standing in front of a group of students, delivering a lesson or lecture, is for the most part simply talking at the students, yet this is not a common method of human communication. For the most part the process of living consists of communicating with other people either singly or in large or small groups. As everyone knows communicating with other people is not simply a question of talking at them; it involves interaction with them and an understanding of how they receive your message. One way of approaching and understanding others is to consider what your reactions are to the communication of others. From this you have a basis for thinking about the views people have about your communications with them. This is not to say that others will feel exactly as you do, but rather they have a range of possible feelings and reactions, some of which will be similar to your own.

Maslow (1962) provides us with more clues when he lists the 13 characteristics associated with healthy people. These show the range of things to look for within ourselves and the characteristics which we can assume are present to some extent in those people we meet and communicate with. They are:

1. a superior perception of reality
2. an increased acceptance of self, of others and of nature
3. an increased spontaneity
4. an increased ability to focus on problems presented
5. an increased detachment and desire for privacy
6. an increased autonomy and resistance to indoctrination
7. a greater freshness of appreciation and richness of emotional reaction
8. a higher frequency of peak experiences
9. an increased identification with the human species

10. improved interpersonal relations
11. a more democratic character structure
12. a greatly increased creativeness
13. changes in value system.

Basically, someone who fits this description is a completely self-directed individual who accepts himself and others and is open to experience and ideas. How do you measure up to it? How do you think those people you meet measure up to it? How will the ways in which they differ affect the way they communicate to you and the way in which they receive your communication?

Take more conscious notice of how people react to your communications in everyday life. Extend this to how students react to your teaching. When you begin to examine this consciously you will be surprised at the insights you receive, both with regard to your behaviour towards others and to the way in which you can improve your communication, not only with students but with all those with whom you come into contact every day. This examination of factors will be continued in Chapter 6, which is concerned with Verbal and Non-Verbal Communication.

Group Processes

A formal lecture can be defined as a teacher standing in front of thirty or more students delivering what is largely an uninterrupted discourse for 30 minutes or more. In a group session, however, the teacher takes a much more subsidiary role. The main idea of group sessions is that the students should talk. Whereas communication in formal teaching is largely

Teacher ⟶ Student

in the group situation it is more

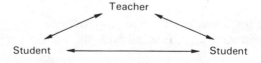

Teacher

Student ⟷ Student

Group work is for the most part a means of encouraging discussion between students. Students should be able to say what they feel and think in groups in order that they can share their ideas and ideals with others. Used in this way group work is valuable for students inasmuch as they are able to see not only the way in which other people regard information but also how they interpret it. This helps students to recognise that because people differ in their reception of a communication there may as a result be points for and against some course of action or argument which up until then they had thought was clearcut. Being able to talk freely in a group also helps a student to put ideas into words and therefore to examine them in a more objective way.

The four main stages in group formation have been described as (a) forming, (b) rebelling, (c) norming, and (d) co-operating (Argyle, 1967). Let us consider each one of them in turn.

Forming

At first, few, if any, members of a group may be known to each other; and as a consequence of this there is the probable anxiety of having to 'tune in' to other people, and of having to find out how they will react to each other. Then there is the task for which the group itself came into being. This may promote feelings of inadequacy in certain members of the group who feel unable to tackle this situation. There can also be anxiety about the ground rules of the situation and how the group is expected to operate. When the group is still in the process of forming, while people are finding out about each other and about the situation they are in, the individual members are subjected to a number of pressures and uncertainties.

Rebelling

If the group continues to meet, members will be getting to know each other, and perhaps testing each other out. Some will try to adopt a leadership role, others the role of follower. Conflicts will be set up both between individual members and possibly between subgroups within the main group. There will also be a testing out and perhaps a rebellion against the nature of the task and the rules of the group.

Norming

When group members begin to know each other, and begin to accept each other and themselves in the roles they find most comfortable and acceptable to other members of the group, then the third stage has come into being. At this point the group forms an inner stability, conflicts are largely resolved, and the group will come to have its own, acceptable norms of behaviour.

Co-operating

With conflicts resolved, the group develops a cohesiveness and turns its co-ordinated energy to the solution of problems associated with the task in hand.

This is, for the most part, an idealised picture of the development of group co-operation, since the continued stability of the group obviously depends on the maintenance of a variety of factors. Group satisfaction is one such factor, since the group generally meets for a specified purpose, the members of the group will continue to derive satisfaction only if they feel that the task is being achieved. One related point is how close members feel to the centre of activities. People on the edge of a group's activities often feel that they are getting little or no information on the workings of the group, and think that they have little say in its operation. When the group develops cohesiveness, members are likely to be supportive of each other rather than in conflict and tend to reject threats to their existence from outside. In a cohesive group there is good communication between members, and the role of the leader is important.

For a fuller account of the characteristics of groups, see *Learning in Groups* (Jaques, 1984). In his discussion of the many purposes in the formation of groups, Jaques lists among them the pooling of resources, making decisions, having mutual support, sharing ideas and creating something. He cites as the unique feature of learning groups the presence of the teacher (tutor) 'who is responsible for both selecting the external knowledge, . . . supervising its processing, . . . and checking its use . . . through some form of assessment.' It is often the fear of the assessment aspect of such groups that inhibits the free communication between members of such groups.

Students are often unwilling to expose their ignorance in front of a teacher, or indeed in front of fellow students. In fact, the students often see no value in listening to someone else's opinion on something about which they think they know everything. At the beginning of a typical tutorial, the question asked by a tutor is often, 'Any questions?' and this, inevitably it seems, brings forth the usual silence. This then leads the tutor to take a topic of his own choosing and to give a short lecture on it. Teachers often fail to realise that there are other forms of group interaction which can be used to advantage. Students often fail to realise how valuable group discussion can be. Jaques discusses group tasks in detail and reviews the variety of interactions which are possible (Jaques, 1984).

The following account deals with some of the main types of group interaction, discussing them briefly for the purpose of indicating firstly the diversity of group methods available for educational purposes, and secondly the main purpose of each method.

Brainstorming. This is a small group method designed to produce creative ideas or a number of possible solutions to a problem. Members are instructed to express their ideas freely and in the initial stages not to be critical of any ideas produced. All ideas are written down and are later looked at critically. This method has an advantage in that it can free students from the fear of expressing their ideas to others. This state often exists in the normal group discussion meeting.

Buzz Groups. This is a useful technique which can be employed between two people who happen to be sitting next to each other, or alternatively with a small group of people. Each person gives his thoughts on a particular topic to the other person or others in the group. In this way a quick informal exchange of ideas can be brought about, where students can share ideas, exposing their thoughts in a non-threatening environment.

Case Study Discussions. As its name implies, the group is given a case study, which can be details of a real-life situation or problem or a simplified, possibly fictitious, study. The discussion of the material allows students to apply things learnt in other situations, to develop their critical faculties and powers of judgement;

thus it can make them more aware of the complexities of human interactions.

Lecture Discussion. At the end of a lecture or lesson there is often a point where the lecturer asks whether there are any questions. This is an opportunity for the group, which has probably been subjected until that moment to an uninterrupted discourse by the lecturer, to ask questions on the material presented. A good deal of the success of this depends on the relationship the lecturer has with his students who at an early stage can sense whether a lecturer can be communicated with in this way.

Tutorial. Here a small group of students meet a teacher for discussion, usually without a central topic. This is in contrast to the seminar, which is usually a group who meet for the purpose of hearing a short talk and then holding a discussion on it. The tutorial is the traditional type of group discussion where, as in the lecture discussion given above, the teacher asks if there are any questions. Because of the anxiety of the students not to expose their ignorance before the teacher or their fellow students, nothing is said. The teacher then feels the need to fill what Broadley (1970) describes as 'the gap of silence', and begins to give a mini-lecture on a topic of his own choosing.

The tutorial should be the opportunity for free discussion and for interaction between student and student, and between student and teacher. Only when students have confidence in the teacher, and are aware of the purpose of such a meeting, and know and trust the other members of the group does this method work.

Individual Tutorials. Here we have the one student/one teacher interaction given under the Socratic method in the first chapter. It is often quoted as the most desirable form of interaction because skilled questioning by the teacher can build up complex sequences of learning. The problem in using this method is that it is uneconomic in staff time and in most cases, with even a small group of students, impossible to implement. However, by using self-teaching techniques the teacher can be freed from routine fact giving, and this may allow more time for one-to-one interaction.

Examples Classes. These are more formal than group sessions. The group usually meets to consider a number of questions or problems which it is given. Firstly the students attempt to work through these individually and then later they are discussed by the teacher. Another form of this occurs when the teacher goes through an example and the group then attempts to solve a similar problem.

Syndicate Groups. This can be used as an extension of the Buzz Group. In this method a large group of perhaps 30 students is broken down into a number of smaller groups. These are each charged with the preparation of a summary of the main points of a topic which is under discussion by the whole group. One person acts as a reporter, reporting the findings of the smaller group to the whole. Points are recorded by the teacher and then discussed. Buzz groups can thus generate the initial points, but purpose and structure is given to the exercise through the act of reporting back. These groups can be extended to include literature searches and the preparation of more extensive papers by each of the groups.

The Role of the Teacher in Group Work

The group methods described above have ranged from small groups without the presence of a teacher to groups where the teacher takes an active part in the normal tutorial. The main role of the teacher in group work is to make sure that the purpose of the particular variety of group work chosen is fulfilled. In all methods the teacher should consider the need for encouraging the student to gain confidence in producing and exchanging ideas, seeking and giving help, and being constructive rather than destructive in his criticism.

The teacher should adopt a flexible role in groups in which he participates, taking the role mainly of listener to encourage students to talk, being directive only when necessary to steer the discussion back to the subject or to summarise the point made so that it can be recorded. The chief task of the teacher here is to encourage the students to produce their own ideas, to avoid correcting mistakes unless they are very bad ones, and to avoid dominating the discussion with what are obviously 'teacher' opinions. One should remember that each student will have some information relevant to the topic under discussion, and one of the objects of group work is to persuade him to express this to the group and to himself.

Teachers often use three basic styles with groups of students: the authoritarian approach, the democratic approach, and the non-directive method. The authoritarian approach is the traditional teacher role where the teacher is the fount of all knowledge and dictates all procedures and methods to the students. The democratic approach attempts to provide opportunities for students to think, act, and talk for themselves, growing towards the goal of self-direction. In the non-directive method the teacher tries not to let himself be looked on as giving direction to the group but listens and tries to interpret the group's own ideas and feelings back to it. In this method the group assumes its own responsibility for achieving the task it has been set.

In a group discussion where the teacher is assuming a directive role there are three main responsibilities he has to assume: first, starting the discussion; second, maintaining it; and third, closing it. The following summarises some of the main factors concerned in these three stages in terms of teacher actions.

Summary of the Teacher's Role: Goals and Techniques of Discussion Leadership

1. Starting the discussion. State the purpose of the discussion, identifying the important issues involved.
2. Maintaining the discussion. Make sure that members of the group focus on the problem in hand, analysing it and looking at it from various angles. Try to ensure that several solutions are proposed before they are critically examined. Provide summaries of progress made at intervals. Encourage the group to look critically at their solutions to the problem.
3. Closing the discussion. The issues and solutions discussed by the group should be summarised. Feed back information to the group on progress made in order to show members what they have accomplished. Set the scene for any further meetings.

In this account of groups, I have concentrated mainly on the process of group action and on the teacher's role within this. There are many factors of verbal and non-verbal communication which contribute to group interaction. These are dealt with in Chapter 6 and obviously contribute to the conflicts or friendships between group members. Groups also have the curious property already mentioned of banding together against a common foe. When this happens the non-verbal signals even between members who have previously been antagonists become positive and supportive. In this connection it is important that the teacher is not seen as the common foe if he is to use the main purpose of group communication to the full, i.e. to encourage students to speak out and to examine critically their own and other ideas.

6 VERBAL AND NON-VERBAL COMMUNICATION

In the teacher's interactions with students, both in one-to-one situations, small groups and large groups, there is a good deal of information passing which is not necessarily concerned with the subject content of the material. The verbal part of this is not just the spoken word passing from the teacher to the student, conveying an unambiguous message, as we shall see below. The non-verbal part can also convey a vast variety of messages. Let us consider each in turn.

Verbal Communication: the Teacher's Viewpoint

In a formal lecture or lesson the teacher conveys information to the student either by talk, by demonstration or the use of audio-visual aids. (The latter is dealt with in the next chapter.) The formal lecture is perhaps the most useful example of verbal communication to consider here, since with one teacher and a large number of students there is little opportunity for student interaction with the teacher. Therefore the verbal message must be clear and unambiguous. In verbal communication there is a considerable variation possible just in the use of the voice to vary sound, tone, pitch, rhythm etc.

Sound intensity is measured in decibels. A quiet whisper heard at a distance of six feet may have a sound intensity of five decibels, whereas a pneumatic drill may have an intensity of one hundred decibels when heard from across the road. Between these two intensities there is the whole range of sounds, from very soft to very loud, to which our hearing responds. Over 100 decibels the intensity of sound begins to overload our hearing and can cause pain and possible damage as pop group performers and their fans have sometimes found out to their cost.

Hall has categorised speech in terms of distance between

speaker and listeners, intensity of voice and content of message (Hall, 1959). The following is an adaptation of his categories.

Content of Message	Distance	Intensity of Voice
personal or confidential talk	closer than 4ft	whisper for confidential material
		soft voice for personal material
conversation between two people	4–6ft	normal voice
information for anyone to hear	6–8ft	normal voice perhaps slightly loud
lecture or public speaking	8–20ft	loud voice

Like many things in the teaching/learning process this appears obvious when it is written down, but how often have we sat through a lecture where the lecturer's voice reaches only to the front row? Loudness, like all other aspects of the voice, is a tool which can be used to enhance and improve verbal communication. A deliberately quiet voice at the beginning of a lecture can focus attention, providing the speaker does it deliberately and then increases his volume when the audience's attention has been gained.

Similarly, tone and pitch can be varied, and indeed are varied, in ways of which we are often unaware since one's voice largely reflects one's inner state. If we are depressed, we generally talk slowly, in a voice lower pitched than normal. If we are excited, we tend to speak more quickly and at a higher pitch.

The rhythm of a voice can be varied. We can vary speed of delivery, introduce hesitations, repetitions and silences. Rhythm is something which we think about more in terms of music, where a recurrent pattern and flow of combinations of sounds generally pleases us, and may stimulate our emotions. A random pattern of sounds can disturb or irritate us. The voice, since it is an instrument and can be discordant or pleasing, should be thought of in those terms when students are subjected to large (or even small) doses of it — bearing in mind that a boring or soporific voice can easily lull one's listeners to sleep.

Speed of delivery is important since the student needs to have time to process the speaker's words. Normal rates of speaking vary between 100 and 200 words per minute. A slow rate of delivery can have the consequences mentioned above, boring or sending one's listeners to sleep. In general, it is better to speak faster with clarity and introduce hesitations, repetitions or silences where appropriate rather than to speak deliberately slowly.

Many people are unaware of the way in which they communicate with their voices. The point has already been mentioned that the voice can reflect inner feelings and emotions. Listening to a tape recording of oneself can show these aspects. It is usually a surprise to hear oneself for the first time on a tape recording because, whereas other people hear you mainly by sound conduction through the air, we hear our own voices partly through air conduction and partly by bone conduction through the skull. Make a number of tape recordings of your voice — you can do this quite privately using an audio-cassette recorder — and you will begin to see the great variety of means of communication possible by using the voice alone.

So far in this account of verbal communication I have concentrated on the communication possibilities of the voice, but it is obviously also important to consider what is said. The choice of words and the context they are in carry a variety of meanings with them. For those wishing to pursue the choice of words further I would recommend *Writing English: a user's manual* (Harrison, 1985). Although aimed principally at written communication the author deals with meaning and presentation, facts, ideas and images, and includes a chapter on 'Unseen partners — the readers'. A useful appendix contains a list of idiomatic usage. Further reading is provided by *Straight and Crooked Thinking* (Thouless, 1953) where in addition to dealing with words conveying emotional meanings, prejudice, logical fallacies, difficulties of definition, facts, etc., he includes 'thirty-eight dishonest tricks which are commonly used in argument with the methods of overcoming them.'

Verbal Communication: the Student's Viewpoint

So far we have concentrated on the teacher's viewpoint. The teacher's words are conveyed to the student but it is the student as listener who converts these words into meaning. It is important to distinguish between 'hearing' and 'listening'. Hearing occurs when sound falls upon the ear; listening, however, involves more than this. It involves the processing of the message by the listener, and this can be considered as involving the following.

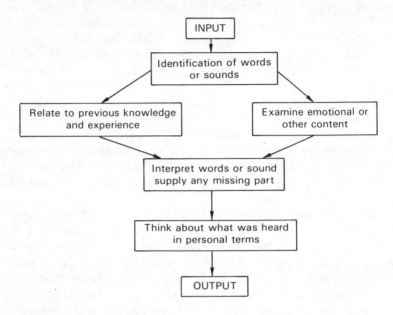

Sounds or words may only be heard indistinctly, and thus the stage at which any missing parts are supplied by the listener is conditional on previous knowledge or experience. This is why verbal communication can often be 'misheard'. Clarity of speech and planned repetitions of material may be important in this context.

In Chapter 4 we were concerned with how the frames of reference built up within the student, and in what way these frames cause selection and distortion of parts of the message. When we hear someone talking, we do not consciously realise the complex processing undertaken in order to make sense of what is being said. As Rumelhart puts it, 'language understanding is an active process involving the interaction of sensory information with our general knowledge of the world.' In *Introduction to Human Information Processing* (Rumelhart, 1977), he illustrates this at length in Chapter 3, 'Understanding Language'. This also emphasises the importance of making sure that the student has sufficient background information to be able to listen. Someone who knows very little or nothing about the subject of a lecture will soon stop listening. There is a definite skill in listening; this involves making oneself interested in the material, something which can be done in a variety of ways. Adopting a questioning technique, as one does when one is reading a book critically, can help. Listening skills can be improved by any method which practises noticing or questioning things about what is being said. Students can be given simple exercises where they are told to listen for certain things in a spoken passage of material, after which they are tested to find out how many things they remember. The advice to a lecturer, 'say what you are going to say, say it, then say that you have said it', is sound, as it helps to direct initially the attention to important things which are going to be said, and then at the end confirms that they were the important features.

Interactive Verbal Communication

So far the kind of verbal communication discussed has been teacher speaks/student listens; but when we extend this to a question and answer discussion or even simply a conversation between two people, obviously the number of possible interactions is considerable. When a dialogue takes place, people take it in turn to speak, and if the conversation is flowing easily there will be a definite rhythm of length of talk for each person, of the speed of reply, the tendency to interrupt etc.

When a conversation is not going well between a teacher and a student, or teacher and students, there is a great tendency for the teacher to go on talking so that the contact between them is not broken by awkward silences. This is done in the hope that it will encourage the student to speak, and once the rhythm of conversation has begun it will continue. Questioning can be used by teachers as a technique to draw responses from the students. Once set in motion the conversation can be shaped into a discussion covering the main points of the subject under consideration. The best way to get someone to talk is obviously to ask an open-ended question, since one which merely requires a 'yes' or 'no' answer or a choice between alternative answers will effectively terminate the conversation.

As we have already noted, students are often reluctant to speak in groups to avoid exposing what they consider to be their 'ignorance'. Non-verbal communication by the teacher can help the situation, it can also be used to control or prevent certain types of behaviour from occurring. Let us now examine this in more detail.

Non-Verbal Communication

When someone speaks he moves his head, his hands, perhaps his whole body. These and other non-verbal signals can give emphasis and force to a spoken message, and may often show more accurately what the person speaking really feels — especially if the non-verbal signal is in opposition to the spoken one. A simple example of this would be agreement when someone says 'yes', and nods his head to show his agreement. On the other hand, if people disagree but feel they must appear to agree, they may say 'yes' but at the same time shake their heads in disagreement. In this latter example, the person speaking may be totally unaware that he is betraying his true feelings by a non-verbal signal. The general emotional state of a person is often signalled by the tense or relaxed way in which that person holds himself. As with aspects of speech other than the awareness of the words spoken, teachers are often totally unaware of the non-verbal component of their communication. This is an important point which we shall develop later. Before doing this, however, I should like to consider some of the main components of non-verbal behaviour.

What is Communicated by Non-Verbal Behaviour?

There are three main areas:

1. supporting or denying verbal communication
2. taking the place of verbal communication
3. showing emotions and attitudes.

Head movements can be used to illustrate these three. I have shown the first area in my previous illustration. The second can be illustrated by the use of the head nod as a reinforcement. Nodding the head as someone else is speaking serves as encouragement to continue. This has the effect of getting someone to talk more. However, if the listener begins to give a large number of small nods, it is probable that he wishes to interrupt the speaker and speak himself. Small, uncontrolled jerky head movements can show that the person observed is in a tense state in which he is unable to control himself. This may occur when someone is in a state of rage. Generally, people who are relaxed will make steady, easy movements.

Eye contact is a particularly important non-verbal skill which should be considered by teachers, since it can close the interpersonal distance between them and their students. When one person looks at the eyes of another, a channel of communication opens between those two people alone. There is usually a heightening of awareness between them and the glances that pass between them can express friendship, love, curiosity or hate. Eye contact can be maintained for a long or a short time, and can be an open gaze or a furtive glance. There are varieties and variations of these. A long, open gaze can indicate friendship or give reassurance. A long gaze may become a stare; this can also create anxiety by indicating aggression or dislike. On the other hand, a short glance may also indicate dislike or deception. If a person is anxious to avoid threats or being found out in some deception, he will generally avoid prolonged eye contact. Often, if a speaker is not looking at the person while speaking, he will make eye contact as he finishes speaking. By this means he is seeking information about how the message was received by the other person.

Eye contact is not the only possible variation, the eye can be narrowed, indicating that the receiver of the message is puzzled or perhaps afraid. The size of the pupil itself can change, for example, one's pupil enlarges when one is looking at something which is pleasurable.

There are many variants and variations which can show non-verbal behaviour; these include those we have already mentioned, that is, voice variations, head movements, eye variations, as well as head and foot movements, nose and lip movements, posture, gait, hesitations and silences, touching, breathing, dress. To give some further examples, let us consider briefly these last two, breathing and dress.

Breathing varies with emotional state and is a good indicator of inner feelings. We tend to breathe faster when we are afraid, when we are in a difficult situation or when we are tensed up ready for action. We breathe more slowly when we are relaxed; when we are emotionally disturbed we may breathe more heavily and yet be completely unaware of this.

Dress is another means of non-verbal communication which is not always considered, and to this can be added the state of grooming of the person. Unkempt hair and a lack of care about dress may indicate a disturbed inner state of a person, while someone neatly dressed with a well-groomed look is probably well in control. Overfussiness can, of course, indicate a tense, overcontrolled state. Generally, dress and grooming help us to see how a person regards himself or perhaps how he would like others to think of him.

We should also bear in mind that these interpretations can sometimes be very specific to a particular culture. An interesting illustration of how variants are interpreted in different cultures is given in *Essentials of Non-Verbal Communication* (Knapp, 1980).

The Teacher and Non-Verbal Communication

Teachers may think that they communicate mainly through verbal means, whereas in fact they also communicate many non-verbal messages to their students. If teachers are aware of the non-verbal components of their teaching behaviour, then it is possible to have control over this. In the absence of a definitive taxonomy of non-verbal behaviour, the best advice one can give to someone aspiring to investigate his own non-verbal behaviour is to read into the subject and to engage in self-observation. The use of video-cassette recorders with a television camera to record teaching behaviour can be very valuable in this connection; many universities, colleges and polytechnics now have such equipment.

It is important that the non-verbal component of teacher

communication should complement and reinforce the verbal component. In addition the teacher should use the non-verbal component to support and help the student, depending on the desired circumstances. The following continuum for non-verbal gestures in the teaching/learning situation ranges from those which are supportive to those which are unsupportive.

1. Enthusiastic/Openly Supportive. Qualities of unusual enthusiasm, warmth, encouragement or emotional support for students or situations.
2. Receptive/Helpful. Qualities of attentiveness, patience, willingness to listen, acceptance or approval; a responsiveness to students or situations implying receptiveness of expressed feelings, needs or problems.
3. Clarifying/Directive. Qualities of clarification, elaboration, direction or guidance.
4. Neutral. Qualities of little or no supportive or unsupportive effect.
5. Avoidance/Insecurity. Qualities of avoidance, insecurity, insensitivity, impatience, ignorance or disruption to students or situations.
6. Inattentive. Qualities of inattentiveness, preoccupation, apparent disinterest; an unwillingness to engage students or situations.
7. Disapproval. Qualities of disapproval, dissatisfaction, discouragement or negative overtones to students or situations. (Victoria, 1971)

When a teacher is working with a large group of students, it is difficult to ensure that the attention of any one particular student is captured and held. Techniques of group work have been considered in Chapter 5, but one of the points to bear in mind when working with groups is that the teacher should try to 'make contact' with each individual member. The teacher should attempt to make each student feel as if the work involves him personally. The obvious way of doing this is to ensure that the teacher speaks to each student and so makes direct contact. However, this is not always possible in a large group and the use of non-verbal communication can be far more effective. Even with a large group a teacher can make individual eye contact with each student. The individual contact can be repeated or used whenever the teacher considers it necessary. Students go out of their way to avoid such contact by busying themselves sorting papers or taking notes. This avoidance of eye contact will occur particularly when students feel that they do not know the answer to a question and are afraid that they will be called upon to give an answer.

The area of non-verbal communication is one which yields valuable information to both teacher and student. Students seek non-verbal cues from the teacher as to the expectations of the teacher and the relative importance of the material being presented. This is why an understanding of the non-verbal component is so essential to the teacher; only in this way can he send out helpful and positive messages which complement rather than interfere with the verbal component. By the same token the teacher can receive much information on how the students are reacting to the material he is presenting. If a student is sitting with focussed attention then he is probably attending to and following the material presented. If, on the other hand, he is gazing out of the window or whispering to another student he may well have lost the thread of the argument.

This latter point is obvious to any practised teacher, but what ought to be done if it occurs? Here we have the limitations of any large group method. Since the teacher is essentially only delivering information to the group, each individual will be receiving the information according to their own particular frames of reference. Some will lose track of the material, others will still be following it closely. Should the teacher stop and repeat some part if he realises some students are not following the argument or should he continue for the majority who are still with him? Only you can judge this in the context of the group you are in front of at the time.

One final point concerning the teacher and non-verbal communication is the need to consider the learning environment in communication terms. The old school classroom is probably the one which will bring back memories and can therefore be best used to illustrate the point. This often consisted (and in places still consists) of a room painted in drab colours with unplanned lighting and acoustic qualities, seats often arranged in rows before the teacher's desk set on a dais at the front of the room. The non-verbal messages from this environment were considerable. The consideration of environmental space as communication is an important part, not only of our formal education system but of our lives in general. *The Effects of the Environment* (Ch. 3, Knapp, 1980) develops this theme.

Further Reading in Non-Verbal Communication

For anyone wishing to read further into specific aspects of this subject, main areas of work by researchers are given below with key references:

Birdwhistell (1952) has been particularly associated with the analysis of non-verbal behaviour; he uses a notational system which represents movements of the head, the mouth, the eyes etc., symbolically. He has also been concerned with movements, for example, of the head and eyes which accompany what he has called 'markers'. Speech markers occur when the fall in voice pitch suggests the end of a speech or when a rise in pitch suggests a question.

Another worker in this field, Scheflen (1964), has been concerned with body posture and positioning. He has noted that postures often consist of clusters of specific body movements, such as holding a particular body stance with the head held in one way for a few sentences of a conversation. The termination of one aspect of a conversation could lead to a further grouping of body movements which are held for a certain period of time.

Hall (1959), an anthropologist, has been concerned more with what he has called the study of 'proxemics'. This is concerned with the distance between people during communication. He has found that there are social norms for distancing, and also that there are considerable intercultural differences.

In the area of eye contact, Exline (1963) has been particularly active. He and co-workers have been concerned with investigating the relationship between eye contact and positive or negative attitudes between people and the relationship between verbal context and visual attention. Hodge (1971) summarises a variety of findings in the area of eye contact in his article, 'Interpersonal Classroom Communication through Eye Contact'. A useful summary of research on the subject is *Non-Verbal Communication: a Research Guide and Bibliography* (Key, 1977).

7 AUDIO-VISUAL COMMUNICATION

This chapter concerns itself with the preparation of audio-visual material used to enhance a direct presentation from a teacher to a group of students or for use in self-teaching situations. The principles of good clear presentation apply equally to both.

In the previous chapter we have been concerned with 'audio' communication under the heading 'verbal' communication. The term 'audio-visual communication' is applied to visual means of communication such as overhead projector transparencies, slides, posters, etc., as these are obviously supported by an audio component in the form of the teacher talking. Sometimes the methods are truly 'audio-visual' as in the case of 16mm sound films, video tapes and tape/slide presentations. In most, indeed all, commonly available methods of sound recording this is effected by using magnetic audio-tape. The following notes refer specifically to the preparation of audio-tape recordings.

Sound Recording

When we were considering verbal communication, we discussed the variations in sound, tone and pitch of which the voice is capable. It is important when making a sound recording to use a clear, non-monotonous voice.

Although the intention may be to produce an audio-cassette version of the tape for final use, it is better to produce the original recording on a reel-to-reel tape recorder. This is important since it is almost impossible to record something without making at least one error. By using a reel-to-reel tape recorder one can edit the tape, thus eliminating the errors. Editing a tape means simply physically cutting out errors and joining the tape together again, using a simple tape-editing block and joining tape.

Making a Master Recording

To make a master recording from which copies are to be made, there are special requirements in addition to those for a normal recording. The first requirement is low tape noise (hiss). The recording process introduces noise on the tape so that a tape copy has its own noise as well as the copied noise from the original. To minimise tape noise one ought to use a high speed tape, high recorded volume and to use the tape recommended by the machine manufacturer. Since mistakes and hesitations need to be cut out and occasionally corrections and pauses inserted, the second requirement has to be ease of cutting. For this, use a high tape speed and record on one track only.

Common faults in recordings which affect intelligibility and the procedure for avoiding them are given in the table below:

Fault	Avoidance Procedure
tape noise (heard as hiss)	use high speed tape, high recorded volume, and tape specified by machine manufacturer
hum	as for tape noise plus ensure recorder is earthed via mains lead; keep microphone away from recorder; avoid mechanical connection between microphone and recorder, e.g. both on same table
distortion (heard as roughness)	do not record at too high a recording volume
inadequate treble (lack of brightness)	clean tape guides and heads before use; use high tape speed
poor acoustic balance (voice sounding distant)	avoid placing the microphone too far away i.e. not more than two feet
excessive sibilants	avoid placing the microphone too near i.e. less than one foot

The rules for making a master recording may be summarised as follows:

1. Use highest speed available, preferably 7½ in sec.
2. Record in one direction only, i.e. one track per tape.
3. Ensure that the record level indicator shows maximum on the loudest sounds, but not more than this.
4. Keep the microphone as far from the recorder as is practical,

i.e. at least three feet.

5. Rest the microphone on a cushion or hold it in the hand — do not lay it on the same table as the recorder.
6. Arrange the microphone-to-mouth distance to be between one and two feet, the final choice being made after trial.

Similar rules apply when recording more than one voice, music and effects. The basic rule is to strive for quality, clarity and accuracy.

Visual Communication

Mere verbal communication is not enough. The teacher's concern is to pass information on to his students as clearly and accurately as he can. He does this by coding his ideas either into the symbols of written and spoken language or into pictorial symbols. These symbols are representations of events, and not the events themselves. Thus, the effect on the student of, for example, seeing and feeling (and smelling) an elephant will be rather different from his receiving a verbal description of an elephant from his teacher. Which is more appropriate depends entirely on the purpose of the teaching. The example of the elephant is often used to illustrate that 'one picture is worth a thousand words', since obviously a picture of an elephant can convey more accurate information in a shorter space of time than many words of description. However, if the teacher were concerned with explaining the drinking habits of the elephant, a film might be more appropriate. The elephant is a good example because, apart from being difficult to obtain on demand, it is really too big to go in the average lecture room.

Thus the teacher wishing to support mere verbal description with visual material is faced with a choice of using one or more of the following:

1. real objects and three-dimensional models
2. pictures and drawings
3. diagrams
4. graphs and charts

2, 3 and 4 can be displayed by a variety of methods, ranging from the blackboard to 35mm slides, video recordings, computers etc.

Real Objects and Models

Allowing students to view real objects can be valuable, especially when they are set in their own environment. Our educational system is such, however, that it is difficult for students to go out from the classroom or lecture room at will. Therefore, these things or some representation of them must usually come to the student. Whereas real objects may be too large or too small or too difficult to bring to the students, three-dimensional models can be made a convenient size.

Pictures and Drawings

Often a picture or drawing will be sufficient representation. A projected 35mm colour slide has the advantage over a model as it can be projected to a variety of sizes. Models are of a fixed size and are often intended more for individual use than group viewing. If different aspects of the object are required, several pictures can be prepared showing the object from different angles. Holographic projections are now also possible.

Drawings have the advantage over photographs of real objects in that they can be simplified to focus attention on specific areas or facets of the real thing. However, if some feeling for the real object is desired, bear in mind that these drawings are a step further away from that desire.

Diagrams

The diagram is an even greater step away from reality, but it is extremely useful in showing the way in which things work and the way in which the parts of an object interrelate to make the whole. Diagrams are capable of considerable simplification, and are of great use in describing complex operations by breaking them down into simpler units of material.

Graphs and Charts

Graphs and charts are a further abstraction, but are particularly useful for showing selected values from tables of data, so that trends in the data can be shown clearly. This point, together with others relating to the choice of textual and diagrammatic material, will be taken up again later in this chapter.

An additional factor which has not yet been mentioned is that pictures, diagrams, charts and graphs can be either static or moving, depending on the choice of media, e.g. by using 35mm slide projection, ciné film, video tape or computer. Advantages and disadvantages of these are given below.

Visual Communication: the Equipment

No equipment is needed to show real objects and three-dimensional models. However, unless the still pictures or visual symbols are shown in the form of printed pages, some equipment, often quite expensive, is needed to display the visual image. There are a number of books which describe this equipment in great detail, for example, *AV Instructional Technology: Media and Methods* (Brown, Lewis and Harcleroad, 1983).

The following lists some of the main types of equipment for the display of visual images under three headings:

1. Still Visuals
2. Moving Visuals
3. Combinations

To avoid lengthy descriptions at this point it is assumed that the equipment is known to the reader. Should more information be required, any standard book on audio-visual equipment, including the one given above should supply it.

Still Visuals

(a) Blackboard, various display boards, posters and wall charts. These have an advantage in that they can be easily used to display either a small amount or a large amount of information. They can be used to show information for a short time or can be left set up so that the information can be studied over a longer period. These examples of 'still visuals' are not properly 'equipment' but have been included here for completeness and as a reference point.

(b) The overhead projector. This can be for immediate use as a 'blackboard' substitute in a classroom situation, but its real advantage lies in its use with pre-prepared material. Transparencies can also be prepared which show a basic visual which can be built up by overlays to a more complex display.

(c) The 35mm slide projector. This can show any of the material used by the methods above, but 35mm slides require preparation. One of its chief uses is to show good quality colour pictures of real objects. It can also be used to enlarge the very small or reduce the very large in size. It can project slides of any of the types of material mentioned in this chapter, that is, pictures, drawings, diagrams, graphs and charts.

Moving Visuals

(a) Ciné film. The type usually used for educational purposes is 8mm or 16mm. This can be used to project sequences of movement of real objects or it can be used for applications of (i) slow motion, e.g. to analyse an athlete's movements; (ii) high speed, e.g. to slow down fast events like the passage of a flame through a combustion tube; (iii) time-lapse photography to render visible movements which otherwise would occur too slowly to be observed, e.g. the opening of a flower; (iv) animation of diagrams, charts, or graphs, e.g. to show an animated diagram of the circulation of the blood.

(b) Video recordings. These are replacing the use of ciné film in education as the equipment is more convenient to use, and video tapes of a large variety of subjects are now available. A television camera in conjunction with a video-recorder can be used to make educational recordings. See *Video Production in Educational Training* (Elliott, 1984) for more details. Video recordings suffer from the disadvantage that the resultant picture is not of the high resolution and quality that is possible with film.

Combinations

(a) Tape/slide. This combination of 35mm slides and audio-tape enables the slide projector to be used not only for still picture sequences but also 'animated' displays including, when multiple projectors are used, a variety of 'fade-in/fade-out' techniques.

(b) Micro-computers. This is perhaps the most important development in recent years. Micro-computers can be programmed to give a large variety of learning sequences involving still and animated pictures. These sequences can be used both to teach and for assessment purposes. In addition, micro-computers can be linked to audio-tape and video-tape recordings to form a very flexible combination of audio-visual presentations. At present, its main disadvantage is, perhaps, the small screen size, and its essentially individual character.

Perception and Reality

When preparing visual material one must realise that what is actually communicated is not always what the teacher intended. The well-known Müller-Lyer illusion is shown below

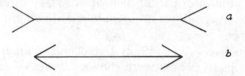

This consists of two horizontal lines of the same length. One line (a) has diverging arrowheads at each end of the line, the other (b) has converging arrowheads. To most people line (a) appears longer than line (b).

This serves to illustrate the point that what the teacher thinks he is communicating may not always be what is received by the student. There is not necessarily a straightforward one-to-one relationship between what the student receives and what he perceives. What he actually perceives will depend both on what he is directed to see by the teacher, and also on the internal frame of reference to which he relates the image. This can be illustrated by a further optical illusion where what is seen is either two faces, or a vase or pedestal, depending on what you are directed to see.

A form of this illusion, together with many other optical illusions and their possible explanations, are given in an excellent book by Tolansky (1964) if anyone should wish to explore this area further.

There are two levels of visual communication which must be considered. The first is that discussed above, where the teacher directs the student's attention to what the picture represents — the level of conscious appreciation. The second is the unconscious level, where the visual material is being assimilated by the student but at the same time being subjected to inspection in the light of all the previous experience of that individual.

All visual information comes to us via the eyes, impinging on the retina and causing changes in the sensory cells. These changes, in the form of electrical impulses, are then carried to the brain, where they are subjected to some form of encoding process to preserve the information. It is at this stage of encoding that the information is subject to possible modification through previous experience.

Carmichael *et al.*, (1932) give details of an experiment where two groups of people were shown a series of simple drawings. As these drawings were shown, one group was given one set of descriptive names, and the other another set of names, which could also have been applied to the drawings. The groups were then asked to draw what they had seen. In a very large number of cases the descriptive name actually influenced the drawing. The people participating in the experiment were being 'told' what they could see and were modifying their perceptions in accordance with their previous experience of the objects they thought they saw. For example, the stimulus drawing might be

the group given the name 'crescent moon' tending to produce it as while the group given the name 'letter C' reproducing it as

(Abercrombie, 1969)

These points of perception and reality should be borne firmly in mind when preparing visual material.

Preparation of Visual Material

The teacher is concerned with passing on information to his students as clearly and as accurately as he can so that the student may have the maximum chance of receiving it. The following account uses the categories which were listed earlier in the chapter, namely, real objects and models, pictures and drawings, diagrams, graphs and charts, and looks at some of the main points concerning the need for clarity and accuracy of representation.

1. Real Objects and Models

One is tempted to say that because a real object is a real object it is bound to present itself clearly and accurately. This, however, assumes that when viewing a real object the student knows what to look for. It is often desirable to prepare students for the real thing by showing them abstractions from reality, a diagram or a simplified drawing, so that their attention is drawn to important detail when they view the real object.

When showing real objects, one main concern is to ensure that they fulfil whatever educational purpose the teacher has in mind. If this is simply to ensure that the student is familiar with the object, either the real thing or an accurate reproduction will serve. If it is merely to show what the object looks like, a photograph may suffice.

Models can retain the complex detail of the original, or can be simplified to focus attention on specific functions. They can be static or have moving parts, and can contain moveable sections to allow inner details to be revealed.

2. Pictures and Drawings

A good photograph of an object can bring an inaccessible object into the lecture room. When real objects are photographed in their normal settings, care should be taken to use a view-point which gives a realistic impression. Distortion of the object should be avoided, and it should be shown as clearly as possible without other non-essential objects cluttering up the picture. Where objects are small enough, or can be removed from their setting, they can be photographed against a plain background.

Drawings have an advantage over photographs in that the viewpoint can be chosen, and any unwanted material simply omitted when the drawing is made.

3. Diagrams, Graphs and Charts

Diagrams, graphs and charts should be clearly drawn. The example shown in Figure 7.1 shows a hand-drawn diagram which when photographed to make a 35mm slide will not be particularly legible. In Figure 7.2 the same subject matter has been redrawn by

Figure 7.1

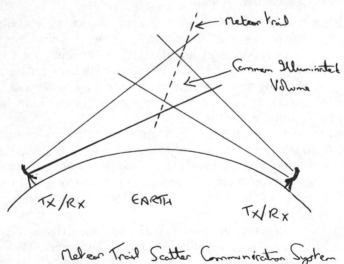

Figure 7.2

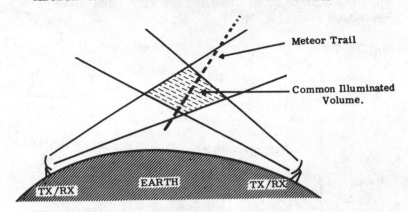

METEOR TRAIL SCATTER COMMUNICATION SYSTEM

a graphic artist. It is much clearer and has greater visual impact. There are occasions, however, when such professionalism is not warranted. The graph shown in Figure 7.3 drawn by a graphic artist, gives added authority to the information presented.

Figure 7.3

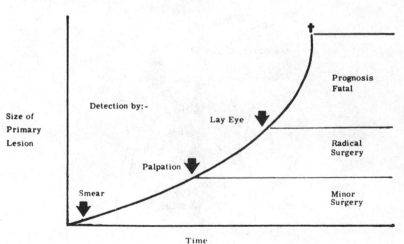

Since the information contained on this graph is not established fact, a hand-drawn slide as shown in Figure 7.4 may be more appropriate in order to make the teaching point that this is a hypothesis.

Figure 7.4

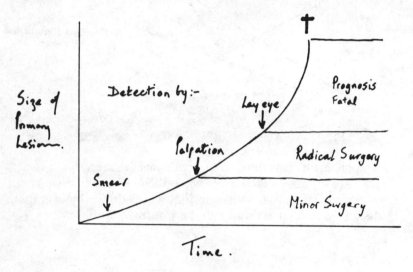

Figure 7.5

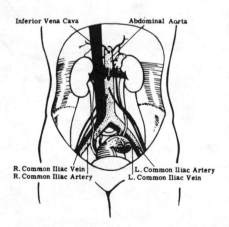

Figure 7.6

Relative luminous efficiency —scotopic vision

λ(mμ)	V'λ	λ(mμ)	V'λ	λ(mμ)	V'λ
380	0·000589	515	0·975	650	0·000677
385	0·001108	520	0·935	655	0·000459
390	0·002209	525	0·880	660	0·0003129
395	0·00453	530	0·811	665	0·0002146
400	0·00929	535	0·733	670	0·0001480
405	0·01852	540	0·650	675	0·0001026
410	0·03484	545	0·564	680	0·0000715
415	0·0604	550	0·481	685	0·0000501
420	0·0966	555	0·402	690	0·00003533
425	0·1436	560	0·3288	695	0·00002501
430	0·1998	565	0·2639	700	0·00001780
435	0·2625	570	0·2076	705	0·00001273
440	0·3281	575	0·1602	710	0·00000914
445	0·3931	580	0·1212	715	0·00000660
450	0·455	585	0·0899	720	0·00000478
455	0·513	590	0·0655	725	0·000003482
460	0·567	595	0·0469	730	0·000002546
465	0·620	600	0·03315	735	0·000001870
470	0·676	605	0·02312	740	0·000001379
475	0·734	610	0·01593	745	0·000001022
480	0·793	615	0·01088	750	0·000000760
485	0·851	620	0·00737	755	0·000000567
490	0·904	625	0·00497	760	0·000000425
495	0·949	630	0·003335	765	0·0000003196
500	0·982	635	0·002235	770	0·0000002413
505	0·998	640	0·001497	775	0·0000001829
510	0·997	645	0·001005	780	0·0000001390

Figure 7.7

RELATIVE LUMINOUS EFFICIENCY
Scotopic Vision

λ(mμ)	V'λ
400	0.00929
450	0.455
500	0.982
550	0.481
600	0.03315
650	0.000677
700	0.00001780

Figure 7.8

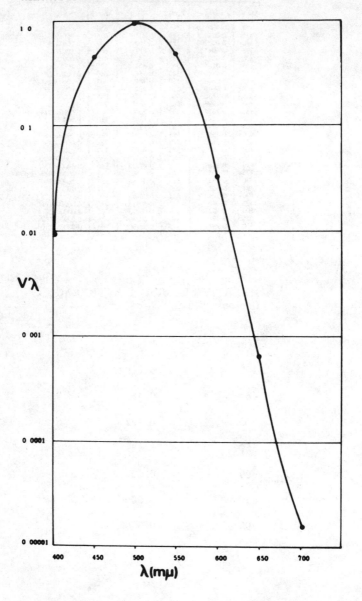

Illustrations taken from books may not always be appropriate for a particular teaching purpose. They often contain far too much information. To make the particular point under consideration, illustrations should be drawn so that only relevant detail is included. Figure 7.5 shows a simplified drawing of the main blood vessels in a human body.

In the same way, when showing written or tabular material, it is important not to include too much information. The table shown in Figure 7.6 has too many details.

If the intention is to show that the readings follow a certain trend, then it is better to use selected readings as in the example in Figure 7.7. In this way the eye is not involved in a mass of unnecessary detail.

Better still, the trend can be shown in the form of a graph, as Figure 7.8 shows.

To summarise:

Visual illustrations should be clear.
They should be carefully drawn.
They should be relevant to the point being made.
No unnecessary information should be included.
Avoid putting too much information in one picture.

The soundest advice for the use of audio-visual media is to use the simplest possible means consistent with a particular purpose. In many face-to-face teaching situations 'talk and chalk' can be supported by duplicated summary notes handed out to the students. These notes should contain main points, diagrams and formulae. In many varieties of group situations talk should be supported by duplicated notes. Where additional visual material is needed, overhead transparencies, 35mm slides, video tape or ciné film can be used.

For self-teaching situations where the student is working on his own, directed references to a book or the use of printed notes may suffice. The audio-cassette recorder allied to printed notes is a reasonably cheap means of presenting an audio-visual communication to an individual student. A tape/slide presentation, in which an audio tape is accompanied by 35mm colour slides, can extend the range of the communication but requires equipment and is more expensive. Video recordings can be used effectively both in supporting direct teaching and in self-teaching situations. Microcomputers can be used in a variety of self-teaching situations.

8 THE STUDENT AS RECEIVER

Although, throughout this book, the student is regarded as much more than simply the passive recipient of communication in the teaching/learning process, nevertheless the process has not, so far, been considered from the student's point of view. This chapter and the following one set out to redress the balance.

Elsewhere, I have argued that the long-term aim of our educational system is the development of the student as a self-directed individual, and not merely as the recipient of various pieces of knowledge (Hills, 1976). The student, however, sees his courses in more immediate terms. What lectures does he have to attend? What assignments does he have to complete? What things ought he to do which will help him in the final examination? These are the kinds of questions he is likely to ask. The 'student as receiver' end of the communication process may thus be seen as an input–output processing model.

Inputs

The main inputs to a student on a particular course are usually:

(a) from the teacher in charge of the course on information about the timetable, the syllabus, various administrative arrangements etc.

(b) course content in the form of a series of lectures or self-teaching material

(c) from the teacher and other students in discussion groups and other forms of group work

(d) directed reading or details of resource materials given to the student by the teacher

(e) information from the teacher to the student on his performance concerning a piece of practical work, an essay or other assignment he has completed

(f) information received by the student on his performance

      in short tests or termly examinations

(g)   informal inputs from other students which help to explain work to a student or give him some insight into the course, which he may not otherwise have had

(h)   reading done by the student, either because he feels he lacks the necessary background or wants to read further into or around a subject

(i)   non-verbal information given largely unconsciously by the teacher.

Outputs

Outputs from the student can take the form of short verbal interchanges with the teacher and other students, presentations, written work or examinations, such as:

(a)   questions, or replies to questions, by the student to the teacher or other students

(b)   student giving a short presentation on a particular topic in front of a seminar group

(c)   completing a written assignment, an essay, report, piece of practical work or handing in a set of completed problems

(d)   completing a test or examination

These are dealt with in more detail in the next chapter.

Processes Necessary for Dealing Effectively with Input

In a paper, 'Self-directed learning for 16–19 year olds', a colleague and I tried to identify the processes necessary for effective student functioning in this area (Potter and Hills, 1976). A list of student needs adapted from that paper is given below.

A student needs to:

(a)   recognise and make the best use of teaching methods encountered

(b)   recognise the value of learning strategies

(c)   predict, plan and organise the use of his time
(d)   know how to listen to, and to take notes from lectures
(e)   create and use a personal 'data bank'
(f)   know how to use libraries effectively
(g)   know how to read books and take notes from them
(h)   know how to prepare for examinations .
(i)   recognise and be able to use good spoken and written styles of communication
(j)   adopt appropriate physical conditions for study including sensible eating and sufficient hours of sleep
(k)   understand aspects of attention, concentration, perception, memory, personal work-rhythm etc.

Many 'how to study' books exist which give detailed information in these areas but many are at the 'hints and tips' level. Very often this may be all the good student needs to brush up his technique. However, the average or not so good student may require more positive help from his teacher, because this type of student may not possess the skills which are needed for him to gain the maximum benefit from a 'how to study' book. Some books go beyond this and in particular *Teaching Students to Learn* (Gibbs, 1981) and *Learning How to Learn in Higher Education* (Wright, 1982) will be found useful for those who wish to read further. *Effective Study Skills* (Hills and Barlow, 1980) should also be consulted as this is directly for use by students, involving them as it does in a series of practical exercises which practise these skills.

The following account briefly considers each of the eleven processes listed: it attempts to summarise their main points so that students may be helped to think about them. The need to think about the way they work is the most important part of any advice that can be given to students. Any student can be shown the main features or ideas, but ultimately it is up to him or her to consider them in their own terms and in relation to existing and preferred methods of working.

Recognise and Make the Best Use of Teaching Methods Encountered

Here the student will be concerned mainly with lectures and group processes. It is important for the student to recognise that the main function of a lecture is to pass information from the teacher to the student. This is in contrast to group processes which allow participation in discussion and allow other views on a subject to be heard.

Theoretically, whatever teaching method is used, the teacher should make sure that students are given the necessary information. If this does not happen, however, the student should always ask the teacher if further information is required. This relates to all other points which will be dealt with here. In essence, a student is not a passive recipient of information but can plan and apply strategies which will help him with the work.

The point made above about asking the teacher is a general learning strategy. If one does not understand or know about something, the appropriate person should be found and consulted. One must, however, be prepared either to get an answer, which is not understood, or no answer, or to find that there is no simple answer. The strategy of asking questions can be extended to the reading of books. If the students adopt a questioning attitude when reading a book, they will find that their attention is focused more clearly and critically on the material.

When preparing a piece of written material or preparing for an examination one useful strategy is to spend some time thinking about the main ideas and trying them in different combinations. This can be done by writing the ideas on cards or pieces of paper; these should then be spread out on a table in various combinations until one is found which seems most appropriate for the task in hand. This is a good revision method because it helps one to think about ideas in relation to one another.

Another strategy which can be very useful is that of working with others. If a student can find a congenial student or a small number of students, it is possible to form an informal group who meet to review and discuss the course work. This has the advantages of the discussion groups previously mentioned but without the impediment that one may be afraid to speak out.

Effective learning strategies are generally those which enable students to be in control of their own learning situation, trying things out, and balancing time, not simply being carried along with the work and often being overwhelmed by it.

Predict, Plan and Organise the Use of Time

Following on from the last point, this should involve the student in taking a step backwards to survey the work load, the new way of life he is leading and its principal features, and to try to reconcile time pressures with the time available. This should involve making a weekly and a daily timetable of work, which should be used flexibly as a set of guidelines rather than a rigid taskmaster. The advantage of organising time is that it can help to minimise counter-productive worry and indecision. By attempting to plan time to cover the known course requirements and by giving time to carry out any written assignments it should be possible to keep some time for relaxation. Another major advantage is that once time is set aside for a task all other things can (in theory) be dismissed and one can concentrate solely on the task in hand. Timetabling can also balance time so that difficult subjects are not neglected. It should be stressed that students should work to a flexible timetable. The main advantage of this is that time available has been thought about in terms of tasks set. This means that decisions on varying the timetable can be based on knowledge of the situation and not on uninformed guesswork.

Know How to Listen and to Take Notes from Lectures

It is possible for a student to appear to be listening to something and yet be unable to remember anything about it. Listening, like most things about learning, demands active participation. Basically, listening is carried on in the mind. In order to engage the mind, it is first necessary to have the basic background knowledge demanded by the course; it should then be possible not only to hear the words said but also to let the mind 'play' with the ideas presented, questioning them, arguing or disagreeing with them and coming to conclusions about them.

Notetaking can help this process, but this depends on the style of the teacher. The teacher should write up on the board the main points of his lecture or hand out sheets of notes. Thus the student will have a basic framework on which to hang his notes, questions, ideas, etc. Notetaking is usually thought of as a linear process, but some students find a 'patterning' approach useful; where the main subject of a lecture is written in the middle of a page and other points and keywords filled into a two-dimensional pattern. Points can then be thought about and interrelated by joining them with arrows as the lecture proceeds. A detailed account of creative pattern structures can be found in *Use Your Head* (Buzan, 1974).

Create and Use a Personal 'Data Bank'

Many students simply take notes from lectures and use these as a basis for their revision in the examination. Rather than perform at this minimum rate it is better for students to adopt a policy of exploring subjects and building up a personal 'data bank', which will stand them in good stead during their courses, and also act as a nucleus for future work. The basic realisation here is that at best a set of lecture notes represents only one teacher's viewpoint. By looking up the subject in one or, preferably, more books different viewpoints can be obtained. Notes taken from books can be used to supplement existing notes, and also add additional points which can be used for written assignments or in examinations. The two usual objections to this procedure are lack of time — an argument which can be countered if time is properly organised — and the possibility of confusion and lack of understanding, if other books do not follow the exact course of the lectures. This latter is more difficult to deal with, since it is often difficult for a student to reconcile different treatments of a subject with the one that has just been given; this is an area where the teacher needs to give help and guidance.

Creating a personal 'databank' is like creating a scrapbook. One should keep one's eyes open for anything which has a bearing on work in hand and either note where to find it or write out short notes for inclusion in a filing system.

It is always useful at some stage to start a card index system. Filing cards, five inches by three inches, can be bought quite cheaply in packs of a hundred. A small filing box and set of alphabetical cards will be needed. Lecture notes, supplementary notes, copies of articles etc. can then be filed in any way desired, perhaps filed in sequence as received. Providing all cards are given a number they can be found easily and quickly by noting their details and reference number on an index card, which is then filed alphabetically by subject. References to chapters in books available from the library can also be included in the card index. Figure 8.1 shows the layout which could be adopted.

Figure 8.1

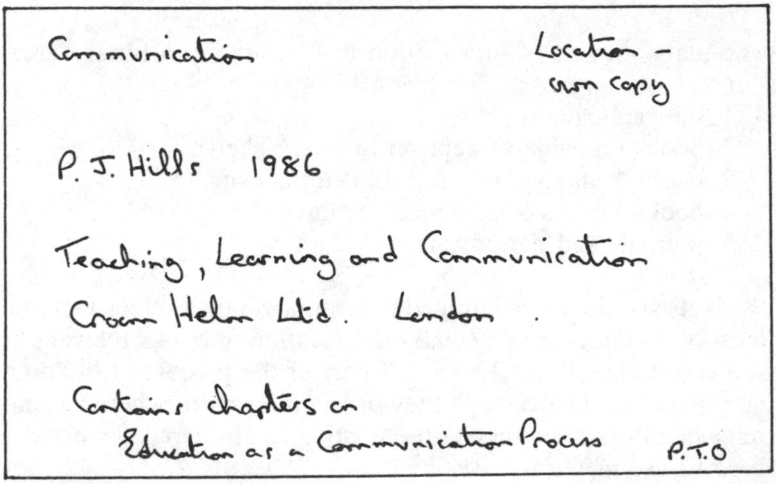

The Student as Receiver

The details on this card illustrate one difficulty. It is sometimes difficult to decide under what subject to file the card. In this case it could have been either 'communication', 'teaching', or 'learning'. With a large card-indexing system three cards would have been the answer, but with a small personal system one entry should suffice. Again, if a card index refers mainly to books and articles on a subject, it can also be useful to file a card under the author's name so that the information can be retrieved from this. Note that the card should also contain summary notes to enable one to see if the reference is relevant to the purpose without actually having to go to the full reference to decide.

As more and more students begin to possess their own micro-computers this filing system can be transferred on to computer. Using a simple data retrieval programme it is possible to access the stored information; by using a number of key words the difficulty of deciding under which category to file the note is thus overcome.

Know How to Use Libraries Efficiently

The main sources of information to be found in a library are:

1. the catalogue
2. books on subjects kept on ordinary shelves
3. books kept specially for short-term loan
4. books kept in a reference section
5. journals and periodicals.

Students should be encouraged to familiarise themselves with the location of all these, especially the location of books relevant to subjects under study. This is all part of the process of building up a personal databank. If they are familiar with where to find relevant information much time wasting can be avoided when the need to use material arises.

Library staff are usually only too happy to advise teachers and students on the facilities of their library. Students should be encouraged particularly to keep an eye on relevant journals both for general interest and for specific references to their subject areas.

Know How to Read Books and Take Notes from Them

Many students believe that if they could take a course in rapid reading, most, if not all, of their troubles would be over. They do not realise that directed reading, that is, reading with a purpose, is more important than what they think of as 'rapid reading'.

The following extract on how to approach a book to see if it will be helpful to you is taken from *Study to Success* (Hills, 1973)

First, open the book at the preface, in which the author generally states the scope of the book and his purpose in writing it. Often, if it is a text book, he states the level and type of student at which it is aimed.

Next look at the contents page. Your first look at this gives you the main chapter headings which show the subject areas dealt with. If you are considering a plan of the book's structure, then the contents page gives you the broad framework, and your later investigations will give you the finer detail.

Now turn to the back of the book and skip quickly through the index. Where a familiar term meets your eye, look it up on the page given and see what the author has to say about it. If you are judging a book which is completely new to you, this is a useful test. With one or two topics which you know well, you can see how the author tackles the subject. If his treatment is poor, then you should be cautious of his treatment of other topics.

In this preliminary survey you should go quickly through every page of the book, looking at sub-headings and chapter summaries where provided. It is possible to go through quite a large book in this way very quickly, not to learn or retain any of the subject material, but to see the author's intention, his broad organisation, and some of the finer detail. After doing this, the book becomes familiar. It is no longer a strange thing designed to stay on the shelf in the hope that its mere possession will help you in your studies — it is something which can be used to help you to further your studies.

The point is also made here that there are many reading speeds which can be employed from fast scanning to locate relevant material down to 'ordinary' speeds which are advocated for reading and learning technical material.

Notetaking from books has already been touched upon in terms of becoming involved with the material, questioning and thinking about the material. The technique is very like that involved in taking notes from lectures but with the added advantage that book material is more flexible. This can be read at a student's own speed, put down and picked up when desired, read and reread as necessary.

Know How to Prepare for Examinations

At the beginning of a course the final examination seems somewhat remote to students who traditionally try to cram their revision into the last few days before they take the examination. However, if students follow an organised plan of action, gathering data etc., as previously indicated, then they are preparing for the examination steadily throughout the course. It is often useful if the student prepares a set of summary notes containing an outline of the main points as the course progresses. This outline can then be used for revision purposes just before the examination. Students should study old examination papers, going through questions, working out 'ideal' answers with others on the course. Adopting a steady approach to examination revision removes much of the last minute anxiety, although it is natural that some anxiety will remain. If revision has been pursued steadily, the night before the examination should be taken off work and the advice is 'early to bed'.

The following advice for 'on the day' is taken from *Effective Learning: a practical guide for students* (Haynes, Groves, Moyes and Hills, 1977).

1. Arrive early, properly equipped.
2. Check the instructions at the top of the paper, number of questions, time, and any compulsory questions.
3. Read the paper twice, taking at least five minutes.
4. On the second reading, make short notes against the questions you can answer.
5. Calculate the time for each question.
6. Choose your best question.
7. Answer questions in increasing order of difficulty.
8. Always answer the correct number of questions.

9. Answer the questions asked, make sure you have covered all aspects in your answer.
10. Leave a little time to check your answer at the end. (Haynes *et al.*, 1977)

This advice is expanded in the next chapter.

Recognise and Be Able to Use Good Spoken and Written Styles of Communication

This involves some practice on the part of the student, but principally consists of advice and guidance from the teacher. See also the following chapter 'The Student as Communicator'.

Adopt Appropriate Physical Conditions for Study

Getting enough sleep and enough suitable food are two essential factors. Eight hours' sleep a night is the usual recommended amount, but this obviously varies with individuals, and the main thing is that students should experiment until they find out how much sleep they need. Food needs are equally variable among individuals, but sound advice is a 'good' breakfast and at least one decent meal a day. The main thing for a student to remember is not to try to save money by cutting down on food, especially fresh fruit.

When students are studying, they either work in their own rooms or in the library. They should be able to work with equal facility in either. Study in their own rooms has the advantage of a familiar environment but the disadvantage of possible interruptions. Study in the library should be in an area near books in their required subject so that reference material is near at hand when required.

The need for timetabling, when working, is important so that practice in concentration on one task at a time enables a student, once in a familiar environment for study, to get down quickly to work ignoring all distractions — at least that is the theory — in reality it does actually improve with practice.

Understand Aspects of Attention, Concentration, Perception, Memory and Personal Rhythms

It is important that students should relate these points to themselves as individuals. This involves the need to realise that everyone has a personal frame of reference for a subject made up from a large number of personal experiences. Related to this is the need to have or to acquire a sufficient background knowledge of a subject to enable new facts, principles and ideas to be incorporated. Students should have the idea of short-term and long-term memory pointed out to them; this leads to the idea that rehearsal of facts either by writing them down or by thinking and talking about them causes the greater probability that the material will be retained in the long-term memory. The actual mechanism of memory is still the subject of debate. A good pragmatic account, however, of the amount of information that can be processed by memory is 'The Magical Number Seven, Plus or Minus Two; Some limits in our capacity for processing information' (Miller, 1956).

Concentration is focused attention. This concentration of attention applies to most processes. It is really attention to detail which includes planning future actions, handing work in on time, etc.

Personal work rhythms should be looked at by every student. Some people work better in the morning, some in the afternoon, others in the evening. Students should be encouraged to think about the time of day when they work best and arrange personal work schedules accordingly. Unfortunately, lectures, discussion groups and practical classes are largely fixed events, but work which a student does on his own should be considered in these terms and timetabled to fit personal preferences if possible.

This has of necessity been a very condensed account of the processes necessary for students to deal with the inputs and outputs of the educational communication process. They naturally reflect my own frames of reference in this matter and, where thought necessary, the balance should be redressed or more detail added by reference to, for example, *Student Learning in Higher Education* (Wilson, 1981) and *Understanding Student Learning* (Entwistle and Ramsden, 1983), as well as books mentioned elsewhere in this chapter and in the bibliography.

9 THE STUDENT AS COMMUNICATOR

Communication is the key to a successful life. People judge others by the way in which they communicate; therefore it is vital that students should be encouraged to be good communicators. We have already seen that some students are unwilling to expose themselves by speaking out in discussions, because they are afraid that they will show their ignorance, experience failure or meet problems which they cannot solve. Their solution to all this is to adopt the role of passive observer, negating the need to communicate with others so that their real capacities remain a closed book. A passive approach to their studies will get them nowhere and is bad training for their future career where their success will depend on their abilities as communicators. They should be encouraged in their attempts and at the same time made aware of the fact that, although an active approach to life and work may lead to some failures, provided that these are seen in perspective and lessons learnt from them, then confidence and success will increase.

The key to the student as communicator is in the development of his or her self-concept. Self-concept is the way in which one feels and acts in relation to oneself and to other people. It is varied and modified by the way people react to one's communication with them.

Let us assume that when embarked on a professional career the student will work in a large organisation, responsible to a Head of Department, but also responsible for other staff. The work will obviously involve making decisions about this group within the organisation and reporting its work to the Head of the department. The work will also involve seeing people from the group, from other parts of the organisation, and from outside the organisation. Meetings will have to be attended at which decisions about the group are taken. Papers and reports will have to be prepared for superiors and for meetings. The situation described is fairly typical of the day-to-day activities of many thousands of people. Students in their later professional life will probably be involved in contact and therefore in communication with people at all levels, below and above, in an organisation. They may be involved in advising and talking to individuals, discussing things in groups and reporting their activities to others. Thus one can see why a good basis for the student as communicator should be laid during the formal education process. The basic elements of this communication are:

1. Interactions with others, individually or in groups.
2. Verbal and visual presentations to others.
3. Preparation of written reports, memos etc.
4. Writing of examinations (this is mainly specific to the formal educational system or for gaining further qualifications).

Let us consider each of these elements in turn.

Interactions with Others, Individually or in Groups

The essentials of these interactions have already been dealt with in Chapter 5. The principles of good group communication can be applied to situations outside formal education. *Learning in Groups* (Jaques, 1984), Chapters 1 and 4 may be useful in this context. *The Psychology of Interpersonal Behaviour* (Argyle, 1967) also gives useful basic information on the conduct of meetings, group behaviour, social behaviour and skills.

Verbal and Visual Presentations to Others

Previous chapters, principally Chapters 3, 6 and 7, contain useful information for the student as communicator. In the context of the student as communicator, when giving presentations to others, all of the principles which apply to the preparation and giving of a good presentation by teachers apply to this situation. A useful booklet on the giving of presentations is *Talking about Your Research* (Dixon and Hills, 1981). Although designed to give assistance to research workers preparing their first oral presentation to a professional audience it contains sections on preparing the script, preparing the visual material and standing before the audience, all of which will be found useful in this context. A section of the further reading at the end of this book gives many other useful references.

The Preparation of Written Essays, Reports etc.

There are obviously differences in the requirements and styles of presentation of different forms of written work. The essential requirements however underlie the preparation of any written or spoken reports or presentation. There are a number of basic questions which need to be answered.

1. What do I know about the subject on which I have to write?
2. What else do I need to find out to cover the subject adequately?
3. Where do I know I can go for other relevant material?
4. Where can I find out where else to go?

Preparation and finding the facts is an essential pre-requisite in the writing of any report or presentation. An account of the ordering of material in this way, with some possibilities for the use of computer databases will be found in my article 'Human Communication and Information Technology' (Hills, 1982).

Once the facts have been marshalled, it is necessary to build a structure for the piece of writing, since it is often impossible to hold the complete balance of topics in one's mind. One should then write a first draft of material, not worrying too much about style or polish. The important thing is to get ideas down on paper. Once this is done, work can begin on the final version, polishing, correcting grammar, style etc.

There are many books which give advice on the writing of reports etc., for example, *Writing Scientific Papers in English* (Woodford and O'Connor, 1976), *Writing English: a User's Manual* (Harrison, 1985). A selection of references to this area will be found in the further reading at the end of this book.

The final version of any written communication should clearly communicate the message which the writer intends for the reader. An interesting account of the communication of official information is provided by Wright's article 'The Design of Official Information I and II' (Wright, 1980). *Designing Instructional Text* (Hartley, 1978) is also helpful in terms of the layout of information.

The Writing of Examinations

This is the one area to which the student probably gives most attention. What the student may not give sufficient thought to is that the examination is a time for direct communication between the student and the examiner. As such the rules of good clear communication should be adhered to closely to ensure that the examiner receives the best possible impression of the worth and knowledge of the student.

The following advice relates to communicating with the examiner when you are in the examination room (see also p. 80).

Read through the whole question paper to determine which questions you can answer best: make sure that you fully understand the purpose of each question you intend to answer.

It is wrong to be in too much of a hurry to get through this preliminary work. Time spent at the beginning of a paper can save you much misplaced work answering questions that have been misread or misinterpreted.

Obviously, when you answer questions, write legibly, try to use good grammar, correct spelling and punctuation. Although an examiner. may try to mark only for the content of a question, a poor presentation with illegible writing is bound to have some effect on him.

Concentrate on each question in turn. Work out a time allocation and stick to it.

Before you begin, work out, if possible, on rough paper a structure for your answer, showing the main points and fitting in sub-headings where possible. In this way you will be able to balance the various parts of the question and be able to keep to your time allocation as you write the answer.

If your examination is of the objective question type where you are expected to select from alternative answers rather than to compose your own answer, then care is needed. There will probably be rather more questions in this type of examination than in the other, but you will still be able to work out your time allocation for each question — and you should keep to it.

The selection of the correct alternative is not a haphazard business, but should be approached systematically and slowly. Weigh each alternative carefully against the original question because sometimes the wrong alternative resembles the correct one. (Hills, 1973)

The Student as Communicator

The student as communicator thus needs skills of writing, speaking and interactive personal and group skills. There are many books which deal with aspects of these, and a comprehensive further reading list for the main areas has been placed at the end of the book so that the reader will be able to go into further details if he or she so desires.

10 TEACHING, LEARNING AND COMMUNICATION

Human communication is essentially a process which goes on between people sharing something with others. Communication is thus concerned not only with passing information, but also with how an individual receives and processes that information. In this book I have tried to show the basic principles of human communication and in what way they are applied both within the formal education system and outside it.

It is by means of communication between individuals that society is able to transmit its values and standards to safeguard the existence of that society. Since the educational process is concerned with every aspect of our society it is both the cornerstone of and the key to our present and future existence.

The formal educational system is under considerable pressure at the moment. Michael Duffy writes of the school system in his article 'Education 2000?' as follows:

> We're punch drunk with change. Comprehensive reorganisations, the raising of the school leaving age, equal opportunity, the Mousetrap-like saga of the reform of examinations at 16+, falling roles, profiles, pre-vocational education, the Youth Training Scheme . . . all have made heavy demands on our resilience and our energy. (Duffy, 1984)

This statement, with suitable modifications as to the pressures, can be applied to every aspect of the formal education system whether it is in further, higher or continuing education. It is perhaps not the change which is the problem but rather the people, the teachers who are expected to implement that change, often without proper preparation or even knowing in some cases, why such change is necessary. These are factors which should be taken into account by educationalists involved in curriculum planning, teacher training and retraining.

Education is by its very nature resistant to change; in the past this safeguarded the standards of society. Now the very idea of society is changing to a more global concept. Communication crosses many boundaries. It is possible in a matter of seconds to reach around the world via satellites to communicate with many countries and many races, each with different traditions, social customs and rituals of behaviour. Education and the education process must change to take account of this. Not only should the methods of teaching and learning be affected but also the whole concept and context of education must be changed. Frederick Williams points out that computers, satellites, tape, disc, microprocessors and new telephone and radio services are 'perceptibly changing the nature of our human environment' (Williams, 1983). The change is not simply economic and political, we are actually in the process of adapting to the environmental change which the present electronic revolution is bringing upon us. This electronic revolution is seen as reaching into our homes and our work, and vast changes are predicted. But what of the effect on the brain and mind of man? McLaughlin writing on 'Human Evolution in the Age of the Intelligent Machine' suggests that machines should become dominant on earth within 100 years. He uses Paul MacLean's triune brain model (described below) upon which to base this assumption, for he feels that relative lack of integration between brain and components makes man a weak evolutionary contestant to machines. In his article he proposes a hybrid organism, or 'hyborg', 'an intelligent machine or network of such machines which has incorporated humans into it as dependent components much in the way that the present human brain has subsumed the brain of lower life forms' (McLaughlin, 1983).

Paul MacLean, Chief of the Laboratory of Brain Evolution and Behavior at the National Institute of Mental Health in Bethesda, Maryland, USA some years ago proposed the triune brain theory. This theory is basically that in its evolution the human forebrain has expanded to great size while retaining the basic feature of three formations which reflects our ancestral relationship to reptiles, early mammals and recent mammals. These three formations constitute a hierarchy of three brains in one, each building on the functions of the other. This theory has a wide currency and will be found, for example, in *Janus: a summing up* (Koestler, 1978) and in *The Dragons of Eden* (Sagan, 1977). As MacLean himself says, the theory is useful in getting a handle on something as unmanageable as the brain. More than this, it shows how nature, rather than disregard and start again, develops and fashions from what it has. Now, as with many things, man has taken a hand in a process which nature began and he is now hastening its development. MacLean in his article 'Education and the Brain' (MacLean, 1978), says,

> In writings that deal with improvement of the external environment, it is repeatedly pointed out how we can 'help' nature. There seems to be a contradiction here: since we are all parts of nature, everything that we do must be considered natural. Nevertheless, if we read nature correctly . . . then perhaps we can help to speed up the process . . . Perhaps it is time to take a fresh look at ourselves and try again to act accordingly.

Carl Sagan in *The Dragons of Eden* (Sagan, 1977) begins by saying 'our children will be difficult to raise, but their capacity for new learning will greatly enhance the chances of survival of the human species. In addition human beings have, in the most recent few tens of a percent of our existence, invented not only extra genetic but also extra somatic knowledge: information stored outside our bodies, of which writing is the most notable example.'

Now of course the computer is beginning to be the most notable example. The computer extends the possibility of our knowledge store far beyond that commonly thought possible some few years ago. The computer can be thought of as man's 'fourth brain' (Hills, 1985) taking its place alongside the other three.

MacLean says

> In its evolution the human brain expands along the lines of three basic patterns which can be characterised both anatomically and biochemically as reptilian, paleomammalian and neomammalian. Radically different in their chemistry and structure and in an evolutionary sense countless generations apart, the three basic formations constitute, so to speak, three brains in one or, more succinctly, a triune brain. What this immediately implies is that we are obliged to look at ourselves and the world through the eyes of three quite different mentalities . . . Moreover, it should

be emphasised that despite their extensive inter connections each brain type is capable of operating somewhat independently. (MacLean, 1976)

There is the realisation that even within our present brain, 'each brain type is capable of operating somewhat independently' and thus even with the addition of our external 'fourth brain' should continue to do so. Indeed, viewed in this way the addition of the computer i.e.

reptilian ←→ paleomammalian ←→ neomammalian ←→ computer

adds yet another set of dimensions to man's potential. However, by its all pervasive nature the computer carries a real threat to mankind unless we heed McLaughlin's warning. Computers can be one hundred per cent perfect, they are very fast (and will be faster) but in their perfection, in their use of the average they neglect the creative spark that is man's very reason for existence. Man must forever strive upwards or he ceases to exist.

Limitless stores of information are theoretically within our grasp. The potential is there and is being used even now. Heads of State, Heads of business can literally at the touch of a button be kept up to date with developments as they happen and extrapolate trends in a way that was impossible only a few years ago. Expert systems and other intelligent devices are being developed now. The next generation of computers will not only store and retrieve information, they will also make decisions, help us to make rational choices etc.

All of this throws into very sharp focus the essential problem of human communication, communication between often sharply differing cultures and the need to take a host of factors into account for understanding and wisdom. It is here however that the potential of the computer lies, with its ability to deal rapidly with a host of different factors, tirelessly and perfectly.

The fourth brain of man is at present, in relation to the other three, as a child is to a grown man. It has the power and the potential but it must be guided to harmonise with the brain and mind of man and in doing so to extend further his power through knowledge to wisdom (Hills, 1985).

Thus, although the present book considers teaching and learning as an interactive communication process, the advent of computers and developments in telecommunications are leading to trends which we as communicators cannot ignore. These trends are considered further in my books *Educating for a Computer Age* and *Educational Futures* to be published later this year.

The first of these shows how the computer can be used to enhance man's communication skills. It explores man's present and future needs and the education of our future generations. The second considers that as information becomes more and more available on-line, so the possibilities in education outside the present formal system will grow. This together with factors like the recognition that a man or woman may have several careers in one lifetime will change the nature of instruction to media packages, computer simulations etc. Learners will be able to access these at convenient times, at their own pace and in places of their choosing. This has considerable implications for the physical location of educational services, and this second volume explores these aspects.

BIBLIOGRAPHY

Abercrombie, M.L. Johnson (1969) *The Anatomy of Judgement*, Penguin Books, Harmondsworth

Argyle, M. (1967) *The Psychology of Interpersonal Behaviour*, Penguin Books, Harmondsworth

Berlo, D.K. (1960) *The Process of Communication: an introduction to theory and practice*, Holt, Rinehart and Winston, New York

Birdwhistell, R. (1962) *Introduction to Kinesics*, University of Louisville Press

Broadley, M. (1970) 'The Conduct of Seminars', *University Quarterly*, Summer 1970, pp. 274–5

Brown, J.W., Lewis, R.B., Harcleroad, F.F. (1983) *A.V. Instructional Technology: media and methods*, 6th edn, McGraw-Hill, New York

Bugelski, B.R. (1956) *The Psychology of Learning*, Holt, Rinehart and Winston, New York

Buzan, T. (1974) *Use Your Head*, British Broadcasting Corporation, London

Carmichael, L., Hogan, H.P. and Waters, A. (1932) 'An Experimental Study of the Effect of Language on the Reproduction of Visually Perceived Form', *Journal of Experimental Psychology*, 15, 73

Cherry, C. (1978) *World Communications: threat or promise*, John Wiley, London

Clift, J.C. and Imrie, B.W. (1981) *Assessing Students, Appraising Teaching*, Croom Helm, London

Dixon, A. and Hills, P.J. (1981) *Talking about Your Research*, Primary Communications Research Centre, University of Leicester

Duffy, M. (1984) 'Education 2000?', *Science and Public Policy*, 11, 6, 364–8

Entwistle, N. and Hounsell, D. (1975) *How Students Learn*, Institute for Research and Development in Post-Compulsory Education, University of Lancaster

Exline, R. (1963) 'Explorations in the Process of Person Perception', *Journal of Personality, 31*, pp. 1–20

Fleming, C.M. (1968) *Teaching: A Psychological Analysis*, Methuen, London

95

Gibbs, I. (1981) *Teaching Students to Learn: a student-centred approach*, Open University Press, Milton Keynes

Gowers, E. (1973) *The Complete Plain Words*, HMSO, London

Hall, E.T. (1959) *The Silent Language*, Doubleday, New York

Harrison, N. (1985) *Writing English: a user's approach*, Croom Helm, London

Hartley, J. (1978) *Designing Instructional Text*, Kogan Page, London

Haynes, L., Groves, P., Moyes, R. and Hills, P. (1977) *Effective Learning: A Practical Guide for Students*, Tetradon Publications, Oldbury, West Midlands

Highet, G. (1951) *The Art of Teaching*, Methuen, London

Hills, P.J. (1962) 'Teaching Machines and Science', *School Science Review, 63*, 151, pp. 604–13

Hills, P.J. (1973) *Study to Succeed*, Pan Books, London

Hills, P.J. (1976) *The Self Teaching Process in Higher Education*, Croom Helm, London

Hills, P.J. (1979) *Teaching and Learning as a Communication Process*, Croom Helm, London

Hills, P.J. (1982) *Trends in Information Transfer*, Frances Pinter, London

Hills, P.J. (ed) (1984) 'Human Communication in an Age of Electronic Revolution' (Whole Issue) *Science and Public Policy, 11*, 6, 334–95

Hills, P.J. (1985) 'Human Communication: through knowledge to wisdom', *Interdisciplinary Science Reviews*, Sept. 1985

Hills, P.J. and Barlow, H. (1980) *Effective Study Skills*, Pan Books, London

Hodge, R.L. (1971) 'Interpersonal Classroom Communication through Eye Contact', *Theory into Practice, 10*, 4, October, 264–7

Howe, A. and Romiszowski, A.J. (1974) *APLET Yearbook of Educational and Instructional Technology*, 1974/75, Kogan Page, London

Jaques, D. (1984) *Learning in Groups*, Croom Helm, London

Key, M.R. (1977) *Non-Verbal Communication: a research guide and bibliography*, Scarecrow Press, New York

Knapp, M.K. (1980) *Essentials of Non-Verbal Communication*, Holt, Rinehart and Winston, New York

Koestler, A. (1978) *Janus: a summing up*, Hutchinson, London

Leith, G.O.M. (1969) *Second Thoughts on Programmed Learning*, National Council for Educational Technology, London

Lovell, B. (1980) *Adult Learning*, Croom Helm, London

MacLean, P. (1976) 'The Imitative-Creative Interplay of Our Three

Mentalities' in H. Harris (ed), *Astride the Two Cultures*, Random House, New York

MacLean, P. (1978) 'A Mind of Three Minds: educating the triune brain', *Education and the Brain*, pp. 308–42, 77th Yearbook of the National Society for the Study of Education, University of Chicago, Illinois

Main, A. (1985) *Educational Staff Development*, Croom Helm, London

Maslow, A. (1962) *Towards a Psychology of Being*, Van Nostrand, Princeton

McLaughlin, W. (1983) 'Human Evolution in an Age of the Intelligent Machine', *Interdisciplinary Science Reviews*, 8, 4, 307–19

Miller, G.A. (1956) 'The Magical Number Seven, Plus or Minus Two; Some limits in our capacity for processing information', *Psychological Review*, 63, 81–7

Mountford, J. (1966) *British Universities*, Oxford University Press, Oxford

Parlett, M., Simons, H., Simmonds, R. and Hewton, E. (1976) *Learning from Learners; a study of the student's experiences of academic life*, The Nuffield Foundation, London

Peddiwell, J.A. (1939) *The Sabre-tooth Curriculum*, McGraw-Hill, New York

Potter, F. and Hills, P.J. (1976) 'Self-Directed Learning for 16 to 19 Year Olds', in *Trends in Education*, 2, 17–21

Rumelhart, D.E. (1977) *Introduction to Human Information Processing*, John Wiley, New York

Sagan, C. (1977) *The Dragons of Eden: speculations on the evolution of human intelligence*, Random House, New York

Sage, M. and Smith, D.J. (1983) *Microcomputers in Education*, Economic and Social Science Research Council, London

Scheflen, A. (1964) 'The Significance of Posture in Communication', *Psychiatry*, 27, 316–31

Shannon, C.E. and Weaver, W. (1949) *The Mathematical Theory of Communication*, University of Illinois Press, Urbana

Skinner, B.F. (1958) 'Teaching Machines', *Science*, 128, 969–77

Skinner, B.F. (1968) *The Technology of Teaching*, Appleton-Century-Crofts, New York

Thouless, R.H. (1953) *Straight and Crooked Thinking*, Pan Books, London

Tolanski, S. (1964) *Optical Illusions*, Pergamon Press, Oxford

Tucker, R. (1979) *The Organisation and Management of Educational*

Technology, Croom Helm, London
Victoria, J. (1971) 'A Language for Affective Education', *Theory into Practice, 10*, 4, October, 300–4
Williams, F. (1983) *The Communications Revolution*, New American Library, New York
Woodford, F.P. and O'Connor, P. (1976) *Writing Scientific Papers in English*, Elsner, Amsterdam
Wright, J. (1982) *Learning to Learn in Higher Education*, Croom Helm, London
Wright, P. (1980) 'The Design of Official Information', in P.J. Hills (ed), *The Future of the Printed Word*, pp. 47–80, Frances Pinter, London

Select Bibliography of Communication Skills and Teacher/Student Processes

(a)   Speaking Skills
(b)   Writing Skills
(c)   Interactive and Group Skills
(d)   Teacher Processes
(e)   Student Processes

(a) Speaking Skills

Bailey, Frances (1963) *Notes for Novices*, Abbey Public Speaking, 83 Portland Road, Edgebaston, Birmingham
Bligh, David (1972) *What's the Use of Lectures?*, Penguin Books, Harmondsworth
Borrell, Peter (1977) *Lecturing*, Keele University, Keele
Brown, George (1978) *Lecturing and Explaining*, Methuen, London
Brown, George and Bakhter, Mali (1984) *Styles of Lecturing*, Loughborough University of Technology
Cockburn, Barbara and Ross, Alex (1978) *Lecturecraft*, University of Lancaster
Cockburn, Barbara and Ross, Alex (1978) *Why Lecture?*, University of Lancaster
Coverdale, Geoff and McDermott, Bill (eds) (1977) 'The Art of

Lecturing', in *Teaching and Learning in the University*, Series 4, Centre for the Advancement of Teaching, MacQuerie University, Australia

Davis, Robert H. and Alexander, Lawrence T. (1977) *The Lecture Method*, Michigan State University, Michigan, USA

Flesch, R. (1946) *The Art of Plain Talk*, Harper and Row, New York

Isaacs, G. (1977) *The Lecture Method*, University of Queensland Tertiary Education Institute, Australia

Gibbs, Graham (1982) *Twenty Terrible Reasons for Lecturing*, SCEDSIP, Newcastle Polytechnic, Newcastle

King, Roger B. (1978) *Lecturing — A RUUE Workshop Package*, Research Unit in University Education, University of Western Australia

Mackay, Colin Neil (1971) *Speak for Yourself*, Gower Press Limited

McLeish, John (1968) *The Lecture Method*, Cambridge Institute of Education, Cambridge

Millett, Wood (1971) *The Art of Speaking*, David and Charles, Newton Abbot

Olbright, T.H. (1968) *Informative Speaking*, Scott, Foresman and Co., New York

Oliver, R.T., Zelco, H.P. and Holtzman, D. (1968) *Communicative Speaking*, Holt, Rinehart and Winston, New York

Phillips, D.C. (1955) *Oral Communication in Business*, McGraw-Hill, New York

Powell, L.S. (1970) *Lecturing to Large Groups*, BACIE, London

Powell, L.S. (1973) *Lecturing*, Pitmans, London

Sidney, E.A. and Russell, L. (1972) *A.B.C. of Interviewing*, Pitmans, London

(b) Writing Skills

Alderton Pink, M. (1954) *Craftsmanship in Writing*, Macmillan, London

Allen, George R. (1976) *The Graduate Student's Guide to Theses and Dissertations*, Josey-Bass, New York

Anderson, J., Dunston, B.H. and Poole, M. (1970) *Thesis and Assignment Writing*, John Wiley, London

Baker, C. (1961) *Guide to Technical Writing*, Pitmans, London

Barass, R. (1978) *Scientists must Write*, Chapman and Hall, London

Bell, R.W. (1953) *Write What You Mean*, Allen and Unwin, London

Berry, R. (1966) *How to Write a Research Paper*, Pergamon Press, Oxford

Booth, Pat F. (1984) *Report Writing*, Elim, Kings Ripton

Booth, V. (1975) *Writing a Scientific Paper*, Biochemical Society, London

Brogan, J.A. (1973) *Clear Technical Writing*, McGraw-Hill, New York

Campbell, W.G. and Ballou, S.V. (1978) *Form and Style — theses, reports, term papers*, Houghton Mifflin, Boston

Darbyshire, A.E. (1970) *Report Writing*, Edward Arnold, London

Figueroa, P.M.E. (1980) *Writing Research Papers*, University of Nottingham, Nottingham

Flesch, R. (1974) *The Art of Readable Writing*, Harper and Row, New York

Graves, H.F. and Hoffman, L. (1965) *Report Writing*, Prentice Hall, New York

Gilbert, Marilyn B. (1972) *Clear Writing*, John Wiley, London

Gowers, Sir Ernest (1973) *The Complete Plain Words*, Penguin Books, Harmondsworth

Harrison, N. (1985) *Writing English: a user's manual*, Croom Helm, London

Imhof, M.L. and Hudson, M. (1975) *From Paragraph to Essay*, Longman, Harlow, Essex

Kirkman, A.J. (1965) *Writing — Science's Neglected Skill: Symposium Series*, The Institute of Chemical Engineers, London

Lewis, Roger (1976) *How to Write Essays*, Course No. E.14: units 1–6, National Extension College, 131 Hills Road, Cambridge CB2 1PD

Lister, T.A. (1976) *Writing for Everyone*, Course No. 411, Units 1–10, National Extension College, 131 Hills Road, Cambridge CB2 1PD

Menzel, D.H. *et al.* (1973) *Writing a Technical Paper*, McGraw-Hill, New York

Mitchell, J. (1974) *How to Write Reports*, Fontana Books, London

Moody, H.L.B. (1971) *Varieties of English*, Longman, Harlow, Essex

Moure, N. and Hesp, M. (1985) *The Basics of Writing Reports*, Bingley, London

Mort, S. (1983) *How to Write a Successful Report*, Business Books, London

O'Connor, M. and Woodford, F.P. (1975) *Writing Scientific Papers in English*, Associated Science Publishers, London

Pauly, S.E. (1983) *Technical Report Writing Today*, Houghton Mifflin, Boston

Padget, P. (1983) *Communications and Reports*, Cassel, London

Quiller-Couch, A. (1916) *On the Art of Writing*, Cambridge Press, Cambridge

Robertson, W.S. and Siddle, W.D. (1966) *Technical Writing and Presentation*, Pergamon Press, Oxford

Robinson, D.M. (1969) *Writing Reports for Management Decision*, Prentice Hall, New Jersey

Rogers, R.A. (1973) 'How to Organise a Research Report for Management', *Technical Communication, 20*, 1, 7–9

Shaughnessy, Mina P. (1978) *Errors and Expectations: a guide for the teacher of basic writing*, Oxford University Press, Oxford

Sussmans, J.E. (1983) *Effective Report Writing*, Gower, Aldershot

Thomson, A.J. and Martinet, A.V. (1968) *A Practical English Grammar*, Oxford University Press, Oxford

Tichy, H.J. (1966) *Effective Writing for Engineers, Managers and Scientists*, John Wiley and Sons, Chichester

Trelease, S.F. (1970) *How to Write Scientific and Technical Papers*, Massachusetts Institute of Technology

Trott, B. (1966) *Report Writing*, Heinemann Educational Books, London

Turabian, Kate L. (1982) *Student's Guide for Writing College Papers*, Heinemann, London

Turner, B.T. (1978) *Effective Technical Writing and Speaking*, Business Books, London

Vidall Hall, J. (1977) *Guide to Report Writing*, Industrial Society, London

Weisman, H.M. (1968) *Technical Correspondence: a handbook and reference*, John Wiley and Sons, Chichester

Woodford, F.P. (1968) *Scientific Writing for Graduate Students*, Macmillan, London

(c) Interactive and Group Skills

Anstey, Edgar (1962) *Committees: how they work and how to work them*, Allen and Unwin, London

Argyle, M. (1967) *Psychology of Interpersonal Behaviour*, Pelican Books, Harmondsworth

Argyle, M. (1969) *Social Interaction*, Methuen, London

Beard, R. (1970) *Teaching and Learning in Higher Education*, Penguin Books, Harmondsworth

Benjamin, A. (1978) *Group Dynamics*, Houghton Mifflin, Boston

Berkowitz, L. (ed.) (1978) *Group Processes*, Academic Press, New York

Bernie, Eric (1966) *Games People Play*, Penguin Books, Harmondsworth

Bertcher, H.J. and Maple, F.F. (1977) *Creating Groups*, Sage Publications, Beverley Hills

Blumberg, H.H. (ed.) (1983) *Small Groups and Social Interaction*, John Wiley and Sons, Chichester

Brandstatter, H., Dans, J.H. and Stocker-Kreichgauer, C. (1982) *Group Decision Making*, Academic Press, New York

Brown, J.A.C. (1963) *Techniques of Persuasion*, Penguin Books, Harmondsworth

Danziger, K. (1975) *Interpersonal Communication*, Pergamon Press, Oxford

Fisher, B.A. (1974) *Small Group Decision Making*, McGraw-Hill, New York

Gode, Winifred (1978) *Chairmanship and Discussion Leading*, Industrial Society, London

Griffin, K. and Patton, B.R. (1976) *Fundamentals of Interpersonal Communications* (2nd edn), Harper and Row, New York

Jaques, D. (1984) *Learning in Groups*, Croom Helm, London

Johnson, David W. and Johnson, Frank P. (1975) *Joining Together, Group Theory*, Prentice Hall, New Jersey

Kellerman, H. (ed.) (1981) *Group Cohesion*, Grune and Stratton, New York

Laver, J. (ed.) (1972) *Communication in Face to Face Interaction*, Penguin Books, Harmondsworth

Mills, T.M. (1984) *The Sociology of Small Groups*, Prentice Hall, New York

Napier, R.W. and Gershenfield, M.K. (1973) *Groups*, Houghton Mifflin, Boston

Ogborn, Jon (ed.) (1977) *Small Group Teaching in Undergraduate Science*, Heinemann Educational Books, London

Payne, R. and Cooper, C.L. (eds) (1981) *Groups at Work*, John Wiley and Sons, Chichester

Palazzolo, C.S. (1981) *Small Groups: an introduction*, Van Nostrand, New York

Sidney, E., Brown, M. and Argyle, M. (1973) *Skills with People*,

Hutchinson, London
Stanford, G.H. (1969) *The Conduct of Meetings*, Oxford University Press, Oxford

(d) Teacher Processes

Abercrombie, M.L.J. (1979) *Aims and Techniques of Group Teaching*, SRHE, Guildford
Bramley, W. (1979) *Group Tutoring*, Kogan Page, London
Clarke, J. (1982) *Resource-Based Learning*, Croom Helm, London
Elliott, G. (1984) *Video Production in Educational Training*, Croom Helm, London
Jones, K. (1980) *Simulations: a handbook for teachers*, Kogan Page, London
Joyce, B. (1980) *Models of Teaching* (2nd edn), Prentice Hall, New Jersey
Gagne, R.M. (1979) *Principles of Instrumental Design* (2nd edn), Holt, Rinehart and Winston, New York
Hills, P.J. (1976) *The Self-Teaching Process in Higher Education*, Croom Helm, London
Hills, P.J. (1986) *Educating for a Computer Age*, Croom Helm, London
Jones, A.S., Bagford, L.W. and Wallen, G.A. (1979) *Strategies for Teaching*, Methuen, London
Lewis, B. and Tagg, D. (eds) (1981) *Computers in Education*, North Holland, Amsterdam
Lewis, R. and Mee, J. (1981) *Using Role Play: an introductory guide*, Cambridge Basic Skills Unit, Cambridge
Lovell, R.B. (1980) *Adult Learning*, Croom Helm, London
Lowman, J. (1984) *Mastering the Techniques of Teaching*, Jossey-Bass, San Francisco
Maddison, J. (1983) *Education in the Microelectronics Era*, Open University Press, Milton Keynes
O'Shea, T. and Self, J. (1983) *Learning and Teaching with Computers*, Harvester Press, Brighton
Martin, R.J. (1980) *Teaching through Encouragement*, Prentice Hall, New Jersey
Millard, L. (1981) *Adult Learners: study skills and teaching methods*, University of Nottingham, Nottingham

Revans, R.W. (1983) *Studies in Action Learning*, Revans, Cheshire
Richardson, J. and Richardson, M. (1984) *Learning about the Teacher, Selected Readings*, Open University Press, Milton Keynes
Rushby, N. (1979) *An Introduction to Educational Computing*, Croom Helm, London
Sledge, D. (ed.) (1979) *Microcomputers in Education*, Council for Educational Technology, London
Tomlinson, P. (1981) *Understanding Teaching: interactive educational psychology*, McGraw-Hill, New York
Van Ments, M. (1983) *The Effective Use of Role-Play*, Kogan Page, London
Yorke, D.M. (1981) *Patterns of Teaching: a source book for teachers in further education*, Council for Educational Technology, London

(e) Student Processes

Apps, J.W. (1982) *Study Skills for Adults Returning to School*, McGraw-Hill, New York
Buzan, T. (1974) *Use Your Head*, BBC Publications, London
Carman, R. and Adams, W.R. (1984) *Study Skills: a student's guide for survival*, John Wiley and Sons, Chichester
Chiverton, T. (1976) *A Guide to Study Skills*, City of London Polytechnic, London
De Leeuw, M. and De Leeuw, E. (1965) *Read Better, Read Faster*, Pelican Books, Harmondsworth
Devine, T.C. (1981) *Teaching Study Skills*, Allyn and Bacon, Boston
Entwistle, H. and Ramsden, P. (1983) *Understanding Student Learning*, Croom Helm, London
Freeman, R. (1982) *Mastering Study Skills*, Macmillan, London
Gagne, R.M. (1966) *The Conditions of Learning*, Holt, Rinehart and Winston, New York
Gibbs, G. (1981) *Teaching Students to Learn: a student-centred approach*, Open University, Milton Keynes
Habershaw, T. (1982) *Three Ways to Learn*, SEDSIP Newcastle Polytechnic, Newcastle upon Tyne
Higbee, K.L. (1977) *Your Memory: how it works and how to improve it*, Prentice Hall, New Jersey
Hills, P.J. (1973) *Study to Succeed*, Pan Books, London

Hills, P.J. (1979) *Study Courses and Counselling*, SRHE, Guildford
Hills, P.J. and Barlow, H. (1980) *Effective Study Skills*, Pan Books, London
Hoover, K.H. (1981) *A Sourcebook of Student Activities: techniques for improving instruction*, Allyn and Bacon, Boston
Irving, Ann (1985) *Study and Information Skills across the Curriculum*, Heinemann Educational, London
Jepson, R.W. (1941) *Clear Thinking*, Longman, Harlow
Mace, C.A. (1962) *The Psychology of Study*, Pelican Books, Harmondsworth
Maddox, H. (1973) *How to Study*, Pan Books, London
Malley, I. (1984) *The Basics of Information Skills Teaching*, Bingley, London
Maxwell, M. (1979) *Improving Student Learning Skills*, Jossey-Bass, San Francisco
Phipps, R. (1983) *The Successful Student's Handbook: a step-by-step guide to study, teaching and thinking skills*, University of Washington Press, Seattle
Rayjor, A.L., Work, D. *et al.* (1980) *Systems for Study* (2nd edn), McGraw-Hill, New York
Tabberer, R. and Allman, J. (1983) *Introducing Study Skills: an appraisal of intiatives at 16+*, NFER-Nelson, Windsor
Thomas, L. and Harri-Angstein, E.S. (1978) *The Self-organised Learner and the Printed Word*, Centre for the Study of Human Learning, Brunel University, Henley-on-Thames
Wilson, J. (1981) *Student Learning in Higher Education*, Croom Helm, London
Wright, J. (1982) *Learning to Learn in Higher Education*, Croom Helm, London

INDEX